10 CRITICAL KEYS FOR HIGHLY EFFECTIVE MORMON FAMILIES

10 CRITICAL KEYS FOR HIGHLY EFFECTIVE MORMON FAMILIES

William G. Dyer
and
Phillip R. Kunz

ISBN: 1-55517-155-9
Library of Congress Catalog Card Number: 94-68445

Published and Distributed by:

CFI
Cedar Fort, Incorporated
925 North Main, Springville, UT 84663   801-489-4084

Cover Design by Lyle V. Mortimer
Page Layout and Design by Brian L. Carter
Printed in the United States of America

CONTENTS

PREFACE

Our original research on strong Mormon families began ten years ago. These findings were published as *EFFECTIVE MORMON FAMILIES: How They See Themselves* (Deseret Book, 1986). Despite the short time span, we believe that an update of the original research is relevant in light of the challenges that these original families now face. In addition, we have found several important keys that can help families of today attain their goals and aspirations of being an effective family–an eternal Mormon family.

What has happened to the original effective families in the time since the initial study? To answer this question, we conducted a new survey. While we did not do a complete resurvey, we did do some follow-up interviews to see if we could identify any trends regarding current family activities.

In the original group, we found the average age of parents was about fifty years old. The youngest parents were in their early thirties, and the average family size was six members. Today, then, the average age of parents is about sixty and the youngest parents are in their forties. The issues facing today's average family are quite different than they were a decade ago. But we found that while issues may have changed, basic goals remain constant. These families, in general, have stayed close to the church and determined to reach that over-riding goal of building an eternal family.

GRANDPARENTING AND OTHER LATER-STAGE ISSUES.

The major change in these families involves the transition of parents into grandparents who face a whole new set of family concerns. Sons and daughters have come off of their missions and now face two critical choices. The first is "What kind of occupation or career should I choose?". Though this question is of special concern for sons, daughters are also concerned about preparing themselves to make a living in the event they don't get married or if they must work to help support their family. The second issue is of vital concern to both sons and daughters. "Whom should I marry?" Parents now find themselves trying to help sons and daughters select a life's work that will be satisfying to them and allow them to earn enough income to raise a family of their own.

Occupational concerns for children are a nagging problem to parents. In what kind of occupation would their sons or daughters do well? Do they really have the capabilities to become a doctor or lawyer or any profession requiring years of education beyond high school? What about finances? Can he or she afford more education? Can the family?

These questions lead to a basic review of parents' philosophies about finances and children-issues that will come up over and over in these years. What responsibility do parents have to help their children financially? Many of the parents in our study came from families that were not wealthy, families that struggled to maintain an adequate standard of living. In their own families, these parents have become more affluent than were their parents. Because of this they may say, "We had to struggle to make our own way. That effort was good for us. Do we do our children a favor by providing monies for them that they do not work for?" Some families answer that question one way, others another way.

Families feel that the cost of everything is so high today they need to help their children financially, especially to get an education or a home. Other families feel that children must be self-reliant and that the effort the child makes to get his or her own education will make the success all the sweeter. Some families loan money to children with the expectation it will be paid back. Others give limited money to children without expecting to be paid back but also expecting children to earn the bulk of their own way.

The whole financial issue is compounded by the even more sensitive matter of marriage. This raises a multitude of complex concerns: "Whom should I marry?" "When should I marry?" A son may ask: "If I marry, will I be able to go to school, or will I have to quit school and go to work?" "Should I borrow money to go to school?" A daughter may ask: "Should I marry or go on a mission?" "What if I don't marry?" "Should I finish my own schooling before marrying, or should I quit school and go to work in order to put my husband through school?"

Hard on the heels of marriage is a couple's difficult decision about having children. "Do you wait to have a family until you finish school?" "Should we practice birth control measures?" "Is that against the teachings of the Church?" "Can we afford to have children now?"

In most of these effective families we have found a great deal of communication and interaction between parents and their children. Our respondents tell us that their older children come to them for counsel about the above issues. Though parents often feel inadequate to give advice and counsel on these matters, they relate their own experiences but often suggest their children get more information from those who understand something about career counseling, talk with their bishop or stake president about family matters to find out Church policy on family planning, and, most important, take their concerns to the Lord.

While the parents are vitally concerned about the marriages of all their children, mothers particularly are sensitive about the marriageability of their daughters. In Mormon culture there is a strong expectation that most girls will marry and have a family. This is seen as the dominant role of women, although there is now a trend away from this narrow definition. Girls are being encouraged to get an education, perhaps fill a mission, even have a career, but to remember that these accomplishments are subordinate to the role of wife and mother.

Mothers tell us that they worry about whether their daughters will date, have boyfriends, have an active social life and then fall in love and marry a fine young man in the temple. The daughters seem to also worry about these matters. What is the age for daughters to marry? There is no "right" time, but parents indicate to us that when their daughters get past the age of twenty-five, the anxiety level begins to rise.

Parents then spend a good deal of energy planning how to help their daughters get acquainted with eligible young men. They also begin to talk with their daughters about the possibility of not marrying, and encourage them to think about living useful, effective, righteous lives as singles.

Parents are also concerned about marriage and their

sons. In Mormon culture, marriage seems to be more the responsibility of the boy. Girls must wait to be asked out on a date. Boys are expected to initiate these social relationships; and if they stay single it's seen more as their own fault. But parents also tell us they do a lot of praying and planning about ways to get their sons married to a good young lady who is active in the Church. Parents indicate that they don't begin to feel panicked about their sons' married state until the late twenties.

GRANDCHILDREN

After worrying through the career and marriage issues of their children, parents tell us one of the next big issues they must face is their role as grandparents. One major concern is: how much the grandparents should be expected to baby-sit their grandchildren. Most of the parents we talked to indicated they want to have meaningful activities with their grandchildren but do not want to be seen as "built-in" baby sitters. However, many parents said that it is difficult for them to tell their children "no" when asked to baby sit. Some parents indicate that they have found themselves taking care of grandchildren considerably more often than they had expected.

Sometimes the children's financial situation is such that both husband and wife must work, with the grandparents regularly taking care of the grandchildren. There are plus and minus factors in this. On one hand grandparents usually develop a deep love for the grandchildren they are tending, but they also may feel they are restricted. One couple, for example, thought they would not be able to go on a mission because of the needs of the children and grandchildren.

Even when grandparents do not regularly tend their grandchildren, there is for many an underlying, often unverbalized dilemma about how much to intervene in the child-rearing practices they see their children using with their grandchildren. They see their children rearing the grandchildren in ways they question. If grandparents see their children as being "too permissive" should they say anything or just keep quiet, wait and worry? Some grandparents fear that if they say something negative their children might become alienated from them, but if they don't, they fear for the well-being of the grandchild.

Most of the parents we talked to indicated they have never sat down with their children and talked with them about the legitimate role they should have with each other and with the grandchildren. Instead, what is used is a kind of trial-and-error method. Grandparents will try one thing and watch the reactions of the parents. They then decide whether to stop or continue the action.

This confusion about the grandparent's role extends to matters about control of children's behavior when they visit the grandparents. Most grandparents indicate they feel the parents should control their own children on such visits. Grandparents see children jumping on beds, climbing on furniture, getting food without asking, creating a mess and not picking up, while the parents do not appear to keep them under control. Parents often feel that the grandparents should set the standard in their homes. This confusion of expectations can lead to some disruptive feelings that may not be worked through.

Finances continue to be an issue for grandparents. Do they spend the same amount of money on every grandchild for various gifts? Is it fair if one family has six children and another has only one? Do you help pay for piano lessons or other experiences if the parents cannot afford such things?

In a wider sense, grandparents' financial concerns include affairs such as lending money to their children. For what purposes? Should they charge interest? Do they put money into their children's business?

FACING RETIREMENT

Families with parents around sixty years old are facing another new condition in their lives–retirement. For some, this period is anticipated as the "golden years." For others, it is a time to be dreaded. The husband may ask, "What will I do with my time?" "Will we have enough income?" Wives may be concerned that the pattern of their marital relationship and personal lifestyle will change when the husband is home all the time.

They begin to ask themselves whether they should go on a mission. Are they healthy enough? Have they enough income? Can they leave children and grandchildren? Basic questions facing LDS couples facing retirement are: Do we have adequate income? Is our health substantial enough to allow us to travel, go on a mission, and do other things we have planned? Do we have enough interests and activities to allow us to feel that we are making some worthwhile contribution with our lives?

For some older couples, there is a concern about where to live. Should they sell the old family home or farm and move to a warmer climate with more comforts in their home? If they move will they be away from children, grandchildren and friends? Will they be able to find a compatible support group? Some comfort lies in knowing they will be a part of an LDS ward or branch; this fact usually means there will be a group of people they can relate to and count on for support wherever they go.

Another nagging concern of grandparents is that of becoming incapacitated and faced with the prospect of living with one of their children. Our respondents generally indicated that they do not plan to live with their children. Many said they would prefer a rest home first. The children we talked to said they plan to take care of their parents if the need arises. This plainly is a condition both parents and children hope does not occur.

Just because a couple builds a strong family at one point in the family cycle does not mean that everything will be smooth sailing from then on. Every phase in a family's history presents new problems, concerns, and challenges. Family members will have to stay involved and be prepared to assist and serve each other and "endure to the end." However, our data indicate that when parents have a vision of what a strong family is like and plan wisely to build a family unit based on gospel principles and sound family activities, their children's families will most likely be able to handle the pressures and problems they face in the future.

Keys learned early on in the lives of these effective families should place them in a good position to solve new problems and challenges as they arise. Of equal importance to those couples we interviewed is the hope that the keys they learned and that were successful for them will also be successful in the families of their children and their children's children. It is the hope of the larger family, successfully tied together and successful in life's purpose, that motivates them onward.

It is our hope that the keys we found in the study of these strong, successful, effective Mormon families will be of value to many other families who were not part of the study, but who have the same type of aspirations and goals for their families. It is our belief that the keys identified within this book will do much to bring about this noble purpose.

WHAT THIS BOOK IS ABOUT

This book is about good Mormon families—families that work. Not perfect families—there's no such thing. We surveyed nearly two hundred Latter-day Saint couples and none came close to claiming they were perfect, but most of them said something along these lines: "We've got a good family. We love each other. We're proud of our kids. We don't have a magic formula, but we work hard at being a family, and we pray a lot about being parents."

Almost every popular magazine rack and bookstore is loaded with commentary on American families, but most of it concentrates on what's going wrong—drugs, gang activity, child abuse, incest, teenage pregnancies, abortion, and suicide. Most reports from sociologists and other family scholars look at the same things. No one, it seems, studies what goes on in families that are trying to be effective and, for the most part are succeeding. What do parents and children do in these families? What factors build cohesion and harmony? What keeps children out of trouble and inspires them to form strong marriages and families of their own?

These were the questions in the back of our minds when we started a research project to find the answers. We think that effective families of any subculture or religion would have most, if not all, of the same characteristics of good

Mormon families; however, we wanted to see how Latter-day Saint doctrines and practices get translated into family living.

Except in Utah and a few scattered communities in the Rocky Mountain area, Mormons are a minority in America. Mormons live, work, go to school, and participate generally in the activity of their communities. Some of the differences between Mormon teachings and national practices seem to be the kind of things that could lead to greater internal cohesion or to potential conflict. For instance, good Mormons are expected to abstain from alcohol, drugs, tobacco, tea, and coffee. If parents follow the Word of Wisdom, and if the children accept it too, smoking, drugs, and drinking are not a problem in the family. If children choose to disregard the Word of Wisdom, however, the resultant confrontations can be even more stressful than in families where drinking might be a health problem but not necessarily a religious issue as well.

Mormons have active social lives as well, but for youth, there are rules that discourage dating until age sixteen, prohibit premarital sex, and encourage marriage only after a Church mission is completed–marriage in a temple with very high standards for entrance. Young Mormons, surrounded by social alternatives, sometimes struggle with these expectations.

Being a good Mormon involves other expectations: regular family prayer, blessings on the food at every meal, church attendance every Sunday for three hours, weekly family council or family night, monthly fasts and donations, tithing, and church callings. Because of Church emphasis on family, many couples expect to have large families that are close, loving, and hardworking. Is there really a connection between meeting all these expectations and having a good family?

To answer this question, we wrote letters to selected stake presidents from a number of states. We received responses mainly from Washington, Oregon, California, Idaho, Montana, Utah, Texas, and Wyoming. In the letter we explained the project and asked the stake presidents to identify fifteen families they felt were "the best families in their church jurisdiction." We didn't define "best families," because the perception of effectiveness itself was something we wanted to study. We specified to them to consider only families who had children still at home with at least one child old enough to be married or go on a mission, because we wanted parents who had worked through the strains of the teenage years with at least one of their children. Interviews later indicated that almost all of the stake presidents used two criteria in their selection process: The families were active in Church and they seemed to be united and supportive of each other.

Using information we gathered in preliminary interviews, we constructed a questionnaire that we sent to approximately three hundred families. About two hundred usable surveys came back. We also held in-depth interviews by telephone and in person with about twenty-five families. From their answers we selected the principles or keys for effective families that are discussed chapter by chapter in this book.

Although these families have "effectiveness" in common, they are very different in many ways. Some live on farms, while some live in cities, like Salt Lake City, Houston, Los Angeles, and Boston. The husbands range in age from thirty-four to seventy-eight with an average age of fifty-two.

The wives ranged in age from thirty-one to sixty-five with an average age of forty-nine. The men have, on the average, sixteen years of education which includes four years of college, although the actual range of completion is from the tenth grade in high school to an eighth year of college. Wives have less education, ranging from ten to nineteen years with an average of about fourteen years. The husbands are doctors, lawyers, managers, craftsmen, farmers, and blue-collar workers. Although most of the women are homemakers by profession, their careers also have included, managerial, secretarial, and blue-collar positions. The smallest number of children is three, while the largest number is twenty-one for the men (including second marriages) and fourteen for the women. The average is a little more than six children per family. In contrast, the national average for couples is about two children.

Is this study representative of all Mormon families? Obviously not. This sample of active families doesn't tell us what a good Mormon family in Germany, Japan, or Peru might be like. We *think* they would be similar, but we just don't know. Families with only one Mormon parent may also be very effective; however, our survey didn't try to find out how. Furthermore, younger parents may have different philosophies of parenting that result in different but equally effective families, but our study was not meant to include them.

We didn't try to get a control group of "ineffective" families, but we asked some bishops and stake presidents who knew their congregations rather well for some names of Latter-day Saints that, in their opinion and for whatever reasons, weren't functioning quite as well. We then did some limited surveying and conducted about thirty-five interviews in Utah, Idaho, and Wyoming, trying to identify some of the differences.

Despite the limitations of the sample, we think the study does give a clear picture of what goes on in most Mormon families with parents who have a strong commitment to the Church and who feel that parenthood is a stewardship from the Lord.

One of the valuable rewards of this project was the insight it gave us into our own families. Both of us had felt that we were the only parents we knew doing certain things; as the surveys came back, however, we discovered that many families had independently made the same connections. We also learned about techniques and activities we wished we'd known about earlier.

Following are each of our personal experiences as Mormon parents and how they relate to our research.

William "Bill" G. Dyer: "Neither my wife, Bonnie Hansen Dyer, nor I come from a traditional Mormon home. My father, George William Dyer, never joined the Church, and my mother, Ada Gibb, was a fiercely devout Mormon. Thus, we seven children were reared in a split family. I never experienced family prayer, church attendance as a family, or a father's blessing. My father was forty-nine when he married; my mother was thirty-two. Because my father was in his fifties by the time the children started coming along, he didn't involve himself much in our activities. Neither of my parents drove, so we didn't go far from our home–a small house with a little corner grocery store attached, located on the outskirts of Portland Oregon."

"Bonnie's family was also atypical. Her father, Clarence Hansen, died when she was six months old, leaving her mother, Wyroa Hansen, to rear four small children alone.

They lived first in Spring City, Utah, but later moved to Provo, where her mother taught school to support the family."

"Bonnie and I met in 1949 at Brigham Young University just after I returned from the Southern States Mission. I was twenty-four, and Bonnie was twenty-one. We were both active in church and had absorbed lessons about ideal family life, but we married without a role model to show us how a active LDS mother and father built a family together. Despite this, both of us desired a good family—a loving, caring, sharing family."

"Our first child, Gibb (William, Jr.), was born at the time I started my first teaching job at Iowa State University. Michael, Lisa, Jeff, and David followed in rather rapid succession, all born in Provo, after we returned in 1955 to teach at BYU. Along the way, we tried to figure out how to be good parents."

"We watched the behavior of families we admired in the branches and wards where we lived, we read books on child-rearing and family relations, and we tried to follow the counsel of Church leaders. This led us to a general pattern of Church-directed activity. We made sure we went to all meetings with our children. We accepted Church assignments and tried to have regular family prayer and family night, but some of the activities in our family just seemed to emerge out of experience. One of our healthiest family patterns was the evening drift into our bedroom, where all the children would pile on the bed with us and rehash the day, shoot the breeze, swap stories, and communicate a lot of affection. We were the only family we knew that did such a "crazy" thing, but I was pleased to see in our survey that most effective families talk a lot with

each other and sometimes develop unusual traditions to
ensure there's time to talk. Whatever the elements of the
Dyer mix, we've been very satisfied with the results. All of
our children have graduated from college, all the boys have
all gone on missions, and all four children have been
married in the temple. We have been blessed with
grandchildren—17 to date. Grandparenting is providing a
new learning opportunity for us."

"Now that Bonnie and I are experiencing the pleasures
and perplexities of grandparenthood, we can look back on
our parenting years with a great deal of gratitude, some
satisfaction, and the feeling every parent has of knowing
there were just a few things we'd like to change."

Phillip "Phil" R. Kunz: "Any sociologist gets used to
people asking, 'What kind of research are you doing? Oh?
Mmmm.' But not with this project. Nearly everyone who has
learned about this project has wanted to know more. Many
of those who participated in the survey went the second
mile and sent us letters and lengthy comments on the
questionnaire. During the interviews they wanted to know
what other families were doing. I shared this interest.
Gathering the data and analyzing it helped me to
understand more about my family, to feel reinforced in the
things we were doing right, and to feel motivated to change
in areas where we needed improvement."

"My wife, Joyce Sheffield Kunz, and I both came from
what would be considered strong, active Mormon families.
My mother, Hilda Stoor, converted to the Church just before
her marriage to my father, Parley P. Kunz, who was already
a third-generation Mormon. My parents were farmers and
ranchers in Bern, Idaho. I was born in the house where my
father had been born, a house his father had built. Our

mountain village was founded by my great-grandfather John Kunz II, who had been sent to Bear Lake by Brigham Young to develop the cheese industry. Even now, only three of Bern's bishops have not been named Kunz."

"My father was one of those Kunz bishops. At the beginning of his ten-year term as bishop, he was promised that if he kept the commandments he would live to see all of his thirteen children grow to maturity. As we brothers and sisters gathered once in 1983 and again in 1985 to bury our eighty-nine-year-old father and our eighty-five-year-old mother, we thought of that promise. The youngest child is now over fifty years of age."

"Our home was one of twice-daily family prayer, missions, temple attendance, tithing, much work and much play within the family. There were spankings, heartaches, and trials, but we also experienced a lot of love. I grew up knowing that my parents supported and loved me. I grew up knowing that they expected me to succeed in something."

"Joyce also was raised in a home of Church tradition, as a seventh-generation Mormon. Her father, Kenneth H. Sheffield, was a member of the General Board of Young Men's Mutual Improvement Association and had been for some twenty years. He was the coordinator for MIA June Conference for many years until the time of his death in an automobile accident. Joyce grew up in a home that stressed family prayer, temple attendance, missions, and service to the Church. Her father was involved in Scouting and with young people all of his life. He worked as a seminary teacher, a principal, and an area coordinator in the seminary system. Wherever we go, we find students who were influenced by him. Even into her eighties and until her death, Joyce's mother, Lucile Beck Sheffield, was a diligent participant in the genealogy extraction program. She, like my mother, labored in the Church all her life."

"Thus, the pattern for our own home was one centered on the Church. We both saw a method of producing a family that had worked, and we tried to bring the principles we had learned separately into our own family. After my army service in Germany, I filled a mission to the Southern States, where my companions and I had several dozen converts. At Brigham Young University, where I obtained a B.S. and an M.S., I met Joyce and fell in love. Our son Jay was born when I was a senior. This event put Joyce's degree on slow-down. We moved to Lyman, Wyoming, where I taught seminary for a year and where Jenifer was born on a minus-37-degree day. Ann Arbor, Michigan was our next home, where I received a Ph.D. in sociology. This was followed by a year teaching in Laramie, Wyoming. During this time we waited and hoped for another child. When Jody was finally born, Joyce's father was almost simultaneously–killed at the height of his achievement. We then returned to Provo where I taught at Brigham Young University, and Joyce finished her B.S. in elementary education. Our family was rounded out with the births of Johnathon Kenneth (spelled to retain the name of his grandfathers) and our last child, Jana."

"Our eldest son served a mission in the Germany Frankfurt Mission, married Rebecca Neumann from Illinois, and is now in graduate school in Texas. They have three children. He was followed into the mission field by Jenifer, who learned to love the people of Uruguay. She earned a Ph.D. in sociology and now teaches at Western Texas A & M. Jody graduated from Brigham Young University as well.

She is now married to Bryan Roberts and they just had their first child. Johnathan served in the Germany Munich Mission and is now attending BYU. Jana just returned home from a mission to Hong Kong and is also attending BYU."

After reading about our lives, you realize this has not been an abstract project. Even though we've been careful in our research and methodology, the subject has more than intellectual interest for us. There *are* some principles that underlie the creation of a good family. For both of us, this project has been personally rewarding. Though one couple comes from a traditional Mormon family and the other does not, the activities and results in both families have been very similar.

The memorable opening line of Tolstoy's *Anna Karenina* is: "Happy families are all alike; every unhappy family is unhappy in its own way." Happy LDS families are certainly not clones of each other, but it is remarkable to us that there is such a consensus. Following is a profile of the characteristics of an effective family. These characteristics or keys are discussed a chapter at a time throughout the rest of the book. These keys appear crucial to the development of strong families.

10 KEYS TO EFFECTIVE PARENTING

1. In an effective LDS family, the first key is church activity and a foundation of gospel values. Many of our effective parents come from strong LDS homes and are

continuing a pattern they grew up with, but a remarkably high number did not have a strong LDS upbringing. Their independent decision to provide a gospel-centered home was enough to make the difference for their children.

2. The second key is love and unity within the home. The parents put their children above work, recreation, and friends. Siblings are more important than friends. Family time is more important than time spent on anything else.

3. The third key is discipline. It grows out of high expectations and clear communication. Parents start with praising and rewarding positive behavior. If a problem occurs, talking it out is the first response.

4. The fourth key is a teaching environment within in the home. Parents consider teaching one of their most important jobs. The church does a good job, but effective parents hold themselves responsible for their children's knowledge of the gospel. Furthermore, learning is an important job for the children, a fact that influences the parents' strong support of public education, discerning attitudes toward television, and good reading habits.

5. In an effective family the fifth key is affection. Hugs, kisses, and verbal expressions of love are common.

6. Key number six is teaching the importance of work and the responsibility of handling money. We found that families use a variety of styles to instill these lessons, including household chores and allowances. What seems important is that all of them do it in some way.

7. The seventh key is a strong husband-wife relationship. After a minimum of twenty years of marriage, husband-wife relationships are not perfect within these families but they're pretty good– rating an average 8.5 on a scale of 10. The couple learns how to make decisions, deal

with the world around them, and handle issues of intimacy.

8. The eighth key is effective handling of adversity. No family is immune from difficulty. Effective families handle floods, wayward children, health problems, aging parents, and money problems in three ways: They seek the Lord's help, they pull together, and they learn to endure.

9. The ninth is a network of family friends and heroes. Children whose parents have friends usually get along well with others and have lots of friends themselves. In addition, siblings have more of an impact than friends, and next to the president of the Church, a member of the family is most likely to be the family hero.

10. The tenth key is family goal selection. Effective families have goals. The parents know what they want for their children in gospel living, education, economic stability, and in their relationships. For the family as a whole, the ultimate goal is "being together forever."

Although successful families are far from identical, nearly all share the characteristics outlined above. In this book we discuss how selected parents felt about their progress at different stages of their children's lives. We also discuss how to initiate change in a family that falls short by using the ten keys mentioned above.

Finally, we take a look at some trends in families, both nationwide and in the Church. What are likely patterns for the future? Can patterns of success be replicated in another generation? Will other techniques need to be developed?

For us and our wives, family living is a great adventure–strenuous, taxing, and immensely rewarding. Our greatest pleasure in doing this research has been sharing with the couples we've met the many insights of effective family living.

INSTILLING SPIRITUAL VALUES

Of the ten characteristics, the single most important and unvarying one is the public and private commitment the parents have made to the Church and to gospel principles. This commitment is the very foundation of their homes.

The last question in our survey asked: "Looking over of the kinds of issues we have raised and any others you may think of, what do you consider has been most important to make you a strong LDS family?" Typical answers were: "We feel we truly love the Lord and are trying to live the principles of the gospel." "Consistent activity in the Church," said a Montana family with children from the husband's first marriage and two from a second. One couple wrote: "The thing that has been important to us in our family is the great feelings we have about the gospel. We know what the purpose of life is; we know why our children are important. Our whole life revolves around the Church. Heavenly Father is a part of us, and we certainly count on him to assist us after we have done our part. We can forgo a lot of things the neighbors have because we know that helping a child to be successful will pay more in the end than a bigger house boat. Missions, temple marriage, and sticking close together—*that's* what's important to us."

When we asked parents to identify the most important positive factor making them a strong LDS family, 96 percent gave one of these two answers–sometimes both. Forty-two percent mentioned the Church and its programs; 54 percent cited personal religious practices such as prayer or feelings of faith. Early in the questionnaire, we asked several questions about typical Mormon activities that many active families would probably take for granted. We asked parents to say whether they always, usually, sometimes, or seldom participated in the following activities.

1. We attend Church.
2. We pay tithing.
3. We have family prayer morning and night.
4. We have weekly family home evening.
5. We attend the temple regularly.
6. We read the scriptures regularly as a family.
7. We accept Church jobs.

The most commonly performed activities were attending Church meetings, paying tithing, and accepting Church jobs. Ninety-nine percent of the couples said they always paid their tithing. Ninety-seven percent indicated they always attended Church, and 93 percent responded that they always accepted Church callings or assignments.

We also gave these parents a list of six goals that seemed fairly typical of LDS families and asked them to check the items that were special goals for them. The goals were:

1. Have children get a good education
2. Have children marry in the temple
3. Help each child develop a strong feeling of self-worth or good self-concept
4. Develop a strong sense of family unity
5. Have everyone active in the Church
6. Have children go on a mission

The first three are special goals of 99 percent of respondents. These goals, in our opinion, are strictly religious in nature. The Church's emphasis on both education and self-esteem have theological bases which are summarized in the well-known phrases "I am a child of God" and "The glory of God is intelligence."

Parents talked about how closely these three goals are connected. "If we could help each child develop a good self-concept, then reaching all the other goals would be simpler," said the parents of five. A father of six noted: "If one of the kids feels dumb or untalented and ends up not doing well in school, even for a short time, we really worry about that and take steps to see that he or she gets some successful experiences. I've seen too many youngsters who feel stupid in school start hanging out with friends who aren't doing well, get involved in drugs, marry inappropriately and too soon, and spend the rest of their lives struggling, never making a good living, never feeling good about themselves, and usually getting a divorce. When kids are doing well in school and are really involved in what's going on in church, it just seems to close the door on a whole bunch of negative possibilities." In their own ways, many other parents expressed their feelings about the interconnectedness of self-esteem, economic security, and Church service.

We also asked parents to identify other goals that they had for their families. Answers included "be happy," "be together in the celestial kingdom," "teach each child to function as a mature, responsible, independent person as early as possible," "have fun as a family." The families in this study also placed a much emphasis on teaching their children good work habits. "Teach them the importance of working and taking pride in what they do," said the parents of nine who run a farm. Other parents said similar things: "Be self-reliant and dependable." "Teach them to work, save money, and be honest."

Lest all of this sound desperately determined, many families listed "having fun together" and "having a good sense of humor" as some of their family pleasures and goals. Mormons have long been known for their industriousness and integrity. It is no accident that these highly effective parents articulate the same values for themselves and their children.

"WE DECIDED..."

We asked a cluster of questions trying to find out where this commitment to the Church came from. We were impressed to discover, once again, the principle of agency. Commitment did not just happen, and it wasn't just programmed into parents by their own parents. It was a conscious decision that can take place at almost any point in marriage. In other words, you don't have to come from a strong LDS family to make a strong commitment to gospel principles, although it certainly does help. That the commitment can be made by any couple is evidenced by the fact that 49 percent of the husbands and 39 percent of the wives had not graduated from seminary. Only 21 percent of the husbands had been on missions. Twenty percent of the fathers and 18 percent of the mothers were not baptized at age eight. Between 15 and 18 percent were baptized after the age of twelve. Some of these people, of course, were people who converted to the Church later in life.

Many parents come from active homes, some are fourth-, fifth-, and sixth-generation Mormons. But at some point—sometimes before marriage, sometimes as a couple—these people decided that their own children would be raised in a gospel environment. For some, the point of decision was very clear. For others, the decision was so logical that there didn't seem to be an alternative. However, they followed it up with action. The action is what seems to separate highly effective couples from less effective couples. One Utah couple with seven children described the process succinctly: "We simply made up our minds, as parents, that we were going to be a strong LDS family and put all our time and energies into accomplishing [that goal]." The father in this family had many, many Church callings. The mother and children joyfully supported him in them. We have tried to teach the children to be aware of the blessings that have come to us as a family for doing so."

For a more extended example, let's look at a couple we'll call Harvey and Joan, who live in the Bay Area. Early in their marriage, Harvey and Joan made conscious decisions to be active in the Church, and when they began rearing their children they chose a different pattern than the one they had seen in their own homes. Joan's father was not only inactive but hostile toward the Church, though her mother felt more support from the Church and encouraged Joan to participate, especially while she was a teenager. Joan's brother was killed in World War II when she was fourteen, and she began seeking religious understanding from that event. When she went to college at Berkeley, she began attending LDS institute of religion classes, where she met and began dating Harvey.

Harvey came from a split family. His father was not Mormon and though his mother was, she was not active. Despite this, she had Harvey blessed as a baby and baptized at age eight, and he became a fairly active member on his own. Harvey and Joan dated, fell in love, and married while they were still in college. Harvey graduated, but Joan stopped her education when the first of their seven children was born.

Although neither of them had learned religious activity from their parents, Harvey and Joan knew they wanted their own family to be different, and the idea of a large, loving family engrossed in Church service appealed to them. They admired the active Mormon families they saw in the ward and were particularly struck by how close and happy they seemed. "Love, respect, and being happy together, that's what we wanted," they said. "We knew we wanted a different family life than the kind we came from." They decided to adopt the activities the Church recommended to reach those goals: daily prayer, weekly family night, regular church attendance, and obedience to Church standards. Harvey blessed the children as babies, baptized them at eight, and usually ordained his sons to the priesthood.

Harvey also regularly gave the children priesthood blessings—administering to them when they were ill and giving them special father's blessings on important events like birthdays and the first day of school, as well as when they were going away from home, leaving for a mission, or marriage. "In addition to the very real blessings that (Harvey) called down on them," Joan said, "I realize now that it was a way of telling each child, 'You're important to us. We know that starting school is important to you. We're all in this together, and we want you to be successful.'"

Harvey and Joan were talented, committed, and creative. From the earliest days of their marriage, each always had a demanding Church assignment. Harvey even served as a bishop. Joan wonders, "As I look back on those early years with several young children, maybe we were too busy, but we seemed to survive successfully. We always felt that we belonged to a group of people who cared about us and our children, no matter what ward we lived in. We felt that our children grew up feeling accepted at church, happy to be there, and happy to help."

Perhaps most important, Joan says, "We tried to live consistently. If we told the children we believed something, we didn't feel we had the right to show something different in our actions. We never asked the children to do things that we didn't do ourselves. We hope that this attitude can carry on in the families of our children and grandchildren."

Interestingly enough, one mother of seven sees the children as having a great influence on the parental decision to be active in the Church. Like Harvey and Joan, she and her husband had both been raised by inactive Mormon parents. They were a hard-working couple, he as county road superintendent and she as school cook after the children grew older. As a couple, they wanted more and decided after the birth of their fifth child to go to the temple. "We wanted what the Church had to provide for our children," she recalls, "but we counted on the teachers to give our children the desire to pray and to do what Heavenly Father wanted them to." They had two more children and, as the children grew older, they made an important discovery. "We had been blessed with seven fine spirits who wanted something in their home that we hadn't necessarily thought about having earlier. We could have filled out the whole questionnaire with different answers, depending on which point in our marriage we referred to."

MIXED FEELINGS

Ironically, we found that many couples in the survey whose family values are inseparably entwined with gospel values feel somewhat apologetic or guilty, because although they are carrying out a Church program, they are not doing it the "Church way" and feel that their families would work even better if somehow they could do it "by the book." These families genuinely want to do everything the Church teaches them to do, and they want to do it perfectly. However, these effective families do not feel paralyzed by their desire for perfection. The statistics and interviews paint a remarkable picture of families being content with family strengths but never feeling they can say "We've got it made."

These mixed feelings should, however, be read in the

light of a historical gap– many of the programs now being advocated for families have come along in the last few years after family patterns were already set. Each of the families in this survey had at least one child old enough for marriage or missions and averaged six children. In other words, the parents are reporting on a busy household where at least some children are working full time or part time, going to school, or living away from home at school or married.

At some point in the future, it will be interesting to see if families with younger children—those who have grown up with this new battery of Church programs for families— have established and maintained a different pattern for the five test activities: temple attendance, family prayer, family night, scripture study, and personal journal keeping. We expect they will do well.

TEMPLE ATTENDANCE

Because of the importance of the temple in Mormon theology, 24 percent of couples indicated that they "always" go to the temple regularly. An additional one-third attended the temple "seldom" or "sometimes." Many of the couples explained their answers, anxious not to have their feelings about the temple misunderstood. It was easy to understand the couple from Texas. They wrote: "We live several hundred miles from the nearest temple. As a result we only go to the temple on certain special occasions. We probably could go more, but it is a major effort."

Other couples are in the same situation. One Montana couple said, "We always go when we're traveling near a temple." Another family plans summer vacations to include a day at the temple. They live twelve hundred miles from the nearest one. Another couple, two hundred miles from the nearest temple, attends "approximately three times a year."

Even where distance from a temple is not great, other activities may take priority. One Utah couple confessed, "Our schedules are so tight that we often have to cancel plans to attend the temple. We feel bad when this happens, and the children know we're disappointed." One father discussed the idea of "seasons" in relation to temple attendance: "We don't go to the temple as often as we would like to, but there are a lot of things going on. When we were in graduate school, we had to study and since that time we have been trying to verify our four-generation sheets in the genealogy program. In our family we think the scripture about the "season for all things" is correct. The season for more temple attendance is not right now. Oh, we go as often as we can—about once or twice a month. We try to go when a relative is married or on other special occasions. My grandparents just about lived in the temple the last twenty years of their lives, which was great for them, but they didn't do that when they were trying to make a living on the farm and raising their children. We look forward to the time when we can go more than we do."

Our view is that attendance once or twice a month demonstrates a substantial commitment, but it does help explain why this family—and probably others—foresees a more intensive season of temple activity after children are raised. Temple attendance does not involve the whole family. Usually the parents go together, leaving the children at home or occasionally, a returned missionary son or daughter, or married children might join the parents on a special occasion. These children are also establishing their own temple attendance patterns independent of their parents.

The temple itself represents an unquestionably high value in effective Mormon families. Almost all of effective couples were either married or sealed in the temple (in a couple of cases, distance had prohibited temple marriage). All want their children to marry in the temple. All show strong support for temple attendance, even though their regular attendance is not as often as one might assume it to be.

FAMILY PRAYER

In addition to temple attendance, another religious activity that is stressed by these effective families is regular family prayer. In this area (and in most others), nearly all of the families described the guilty gap between an ideal they accept and the tough realities of getting through a day.

Twenty-eight percent of the families said they "always" held morning and evening family prayer, and 45 percent said they "usually" did, making a total of 73 percent that usually had prayer together. A common comment was, "We almost always get the family together for prayer once during the day but not every morning and evening."

Also, part of the explanation for all of those who do not

have family prayer may be in the families' definitions of family prayer. In an interview, one father said with some feelings of frustration and resignation, "Given the ages and situations of our children, it is almost impossible to have regular family prayer. Some work right after school until rather late. They aren't here for evening prayer and don't want to get up when others have to be up and gone for early morning seminary. Then when you add in different ones having practices, games, meetings, it just seems the family is not all together to have regular prayer. What we do is to have a prayer when we bless the food with all those who are here, and I know that all of us say our private prayers. But regular morning and evening prayer with all of the family just *seems* to be practically impossible."

Another family that clearly seemed to hold what we would call "family prayer" didn't think they were: "We have family prayer once in a while, but it is hard to do since our children work [outside] the home. We are seldom all home at the same time. We pray with whoever is there— sometimes only four or five us at a time, but that is all we can get together. Sometimes there may just be the two of us or only one of the children with us. On Sunday we can usually all pray together in family prayer."

Family Home Evening

Sixty-six percent of the families said they "always" or "usually" held a family home evening each week, with 18 percent reporting "always" and 48 percent reporting "usually." The remaining one-third said they held it "sometimes" or "seldom."

Family home evening was instituted as a formal program in the early 1960s. Many of the families in our sample had already established other patterns with their children that did not involve a pre-formatted "meeting."

As a result, many of them probably said they were not holding family home evening. "Our last girl is leaving for college," wrote one Idaho mother of seven. "When there were other children at home, we had family home evening and family prayer regularly." But with almost all the children gone and the husband working night shift, these programs no longer seemed to fit the family's needs. Several other families said that the program worked better with younger children than with older ones.

Still, many families spent time together regularly and accomplished many of the goals of the family home evening program. For example, a regular Sunday dinner-table topic would be the lessons presented in Sunday School and Primary that day. One mother wrote, "We spend more time together as a family than most other families we know. We read together regularly—scriptures and other books. We play games together, work together, and eat together." Many families hold extended discussions about the scriptures, problems of life, personal and family problems, and plans for a particular project. One of these families, which seemed to participate in an extraordinarily high level of family interaction, still said somewhat apologetically: "We can see the value of the family hone evening lessons to us. It is too bad that we didn't get those lesson manuals earlier in our married life. I guess we did do a lot of that sort of thing but not as well as the book does now."

FAMILY SCRIPTURE STUDY

Twenty-eight percent of the families in this study indicated that they regularly read the scriptures together. Considerably more hold family home evening than read the scriptures. More than 70 percent of the families said that scripture reading as a family was done only "sometimes" or "seldom."

When scripture study works, it seems to be rewarding. One Utah father described in an interview how they were doing in this area: "Our stake president used to talk in stake conference about how each morning they were reading the scriptures as a family. We felt that we should do it too, but it's tough to find time for it. We talked with the children who are still living at home, and they wanted to do it. We finally decided that we could read for a while if everyone got up ten minutes earlier. We read about four or five days a week now. So far we have read the Book of Mormon, the Doctrine and Covenants, and the Pearl of Great Price, and now we are in the New Testament. We start reading around the breakfast table while my wife is putting the final touches on breakfast, and that seems to work well."

In one family where the father is disabled and the family has been under considerable financial pressure, the mother wrote that one of their greatest strengths as a family comes from "our family mornings where we sing, read the scriptures, and pray together every day."

One Utah mother of six, ages six to twenty-two, who said she filled out the questionnaire alone, noted that the family studies the scriptures regularly. In fact, their three most important rules are: "Everyone comes to scripture study, everyone goes to church, and everyone comes to family home evening." An explanatory note clarified: "Mom sets up these rules, gets everyone up, and prepares the lesson, and Dad comes if he feels like it." Several families said that individual study works well for them. One Wyoming father listens to tapes of the scriptures while he's working. The children play the tapes at bedtime. Another mother includes taped stories from the scriptures as part of family activities. One California family of four reads individually, following the schedule in the priesthood manual. They then discuss their readings together. Still other families try to make scripture reading an important part of their family home evenings. The recent emphasis placed upon the Book of Mormon by President Ezra Taft Benson has undoubtedly had a profound influence on families in regard to their reading of this book and following its teachings.

PERSONAL JOURNALS

Another area of family activity particularly stressed by President Spencer W. Kimball during his presidency was journal-keeping. Twenty-five percent of the fathers indicated they write in a journal regularly, and 45 percent of the mothers said they make regular journal entries. The children's activities in this area are almost the same as mother's—about 48 percent. These results suggest that children reared writing journals as with the family may adopt the practice at a higher level than their parents.

Even though parents feel that they could be doing better at Church-related family goals and work hard to see that they and their children are involved in Church activity, we felt that in no way had they turned part of child rearing over to the Church. Many expressed gratitude for help from the Sunday School, a Scout leader, or an outstanding Young Women leader; however, they saw this help as supplemental. As one mother said, "We are happy for the programs of the Church. Programs seem to come up to help various children from time to time. Nevertheless, we realize the whole (responsibility) is ours. If we fail in our home, we are responsible. If a child goes astray, we can't say that he had a bad Sunday School teacher, can we? That wouldn't buy much sympathy."

Among the less-effective LDS families we interviewed, at least one family functioned very well without much Church activity. Beth comes from a long line of Mormon pioneers and is proud of her heritage, even though her family does not attend church regularly or hold regular family prayer. She met Jim, a non-Mormon, at BYU, and they married. They went to church occasionally, their six children were blessed and baptized, and Jim was also baptized. In their family, they stressed the values of moral behavior and educational achievement, and the children have grown up staying close to each other and mutually supportive. Most consider themselves to be Mormon but are not deeply committed to LDS practices.

Most of the less-effective families that we interviewed have not been able to maintain close ties to the Church. One Wyoming father of five started smoking, then no longer felt comfortable at church. "Things have been pretty much downhill since then," he said. Another couple who had not been worthy to qualify for a temple marriage admitted, "Then, it just got to be easy to stay away from Church." A third couple "just never did get around to" holding family home evening and family prayer although they said they "probably should have." Another Utah mother with three teenagers felt that it was too late to start holding family prayer: "My kids would probably just laugh at the idea."

Couples in our highly effective group, however, are clear about the role of the gospel and the Church in their families' successes. One Salt Lake City professional couple with six children wrote: "Without question, the gospel has been the most important factor in making us a strong family. We don't know how families function in this world without this knowledge and without the influence of the Spirit. We're not just saying this because it sounds good or is expected of us. It is true for our family."

In short, the couples who have made a decision that they want a thoroughly Mormon family have found that personal values and institutional values work together. Their children receive clear messages that affirm their worth, set high expectations, and pay off in feelings of love and respect. It's a potent combination.

MAKING A COMMITMENT TO THE FAMILY

When effective families try to put their finger on what makes them successful, an overwhelming majority mention two factors: (1) their commitment to Church principles and programs, and (2) a mutual sense of internal bonding, a deep sense of love, caring, and unity. Although we've discussed these factors in two separate chapters, again and again parents in our survey linked them. "The Church and love for each other and the children" were the most important values to an Idaho couple. "We have a testimony of the gospel of Jesus Christ," said a couple from a small Utah town. "We *know* why we are here, and the family is the center of that reason." "We love our children and place the success of the family above material success, professional success, social status, or political recognition," said the Provo parents of seven children ranging in age from twelve to thirty-two. Another Utah couple with seven children said that one factor in their success was "spending lots of one-on-one time, letting our children know they are more important than work, friends, or hobbies."

Unity was a concept these parents described in detail with statements like: "We work together." "We're on each other's side." "We help each other." "We're each other's best friends."

A Montana couple, parents of ten, said simply, "Each person has a responsibility to the rest of the family." A mother in Washington with five children wrote, "Being in this family means knowing that when everything else in the world is against us, we can come home and feel loved and know that other family members will show that they think we're special." Idaho parents of eight asserted, "We're all proud to be members of our family." One Utah couple, the parents of ten, even expressed a kind of wistfulness in answering a question about the age at which they found their children easiest to rear. They responded, "Between birth and twelve," explaining, "We were a complete community within our family." An Idaho couple observed, in a backhanded critique of society, "We have been so contented as a family that our children are probably not as outgoing and aggressive as the business world sometimes demands." A mother said, speaking of a strong extended family with actively involved grandparents, aunts, and uncles, "It means something to belong to this family, and our kids know it. Not that we're anything special—well, yes, special—but not exactly."

In our egalitarian society, these parents seemed to be struggling to find the word that earlier generations and other societies would have understood more easily: clans. Without any necessary suspicion of outsiders or any smug superiority, they still sense deeply that being a member of the family—*their* family—makes a big difference. All people aren't equally important. The family comes first, and then comes everybody else. That's probably why so many parents, trying to talk about the sense of unity in their family, resorted in frustration to repeating, "We're a *family*."

In less-effective families, this sense of identity and unity may not develop. One mother of three, whose teenagers had been characterized by rebellion, drug abuse, and confrontation, said bleakly, "We're *not* a special family." What makes the difference?

Family identity may take the form of cute T-shirts at family reunions or a joint family savings account, but these are just manifestations of a deeper source of identity. Parents communicate to children that they have entered a distinctive society by being a member of the Walker or the Thompson family. There's a boundary. They're just different. "Friends are wonderful and great," as one Texas couple, the parents of six, put it. "But families are *eternal*." "The children would rather do things with family than with peers most of the time," observed an Idaho couple, parents of seven.

As a result of communicating a sense of family distinction, parents find it easy to say, "In *our* family, we do (or don't do) this," and children accept it because they understand, even on a level they can't articulate, that belonging to their family means something extra special.

One couple phrased the meaning of family this way for their children: "Families are more important than friends. This means we will treat family members better than we treat our friends. And family activities will take precedence over activities with friends."

Sociology is full of examples of families highly united around rather antisocial purposes—organized crime, for instance, or just endless bickering. In other words, you can be united without being loving. But love is an element that nearly all of the successful families linked with their unity, when we talked to them.

Do love and unity occur spontaneously, or can you create them as a result of certain kinds of activities? The answer appears to be yes to both questions. Feelings of love generate sharing and caring activities. The success of these activities in turn confirms and strengthens sharing and caring feelings.

VALUING CHILDREN

A clear, underlying condition of family unity is the high value that parents place on their children. By society's standards our respondents have a lot of children—an average of six per family. The average American family has 2.81 members, including the parents or parent. Traditional societies tend to value children somewhat as possessions. Some say that the parents of large families have status because children represent sizable financial leverage for the future. Our highly individualistic society tends to see children as unique little planets, orbiting for a time around the parents' sun but soon shooting off into their own space.

These views represent two extremes. In effective families, the value of children seems to lie somewhere in between. Children are definitely individuals, but they complete, enrich, and complement an already existing pattern. In other words, children are seen as both giving something and getting something—that sense of family.

"We put our family life above everything else. We always have in mind that we are going to make it work," said one couple. "Our kids come first," says another couple, "and they know it." A Texas couple with four children from ages sixteen to twenty-four wrote, "We *really* love and support each other. Our family comes *first*. Another couple said, "Unconditional love for each other has got to be one of the factors that makes our family work." In contrast, the mother in one of the less-effective families said with resignation, "My husband has never taken any interest in the children. His activities are always more important than mine or theirs. He's never helped me with anything."

In successful families, nearly every couple expressed how eagerly they anticipated the births of their children and how excited the older children were when the younger children arrived. Naturally, the parents had a great deal to do with shaping those feelings. One couple described how they did it: "Before each of the later children [were born], we would talk with the older ones about the new brother or sister who would come. When the baby began to move in the womb, all of the children would like to feel the movement. It was exciting to them. There were never any phony stories about the stork delivering babies. They all knew that the baby was in mother's 'tummy' and that she would have to go to the hospital so the doctor could help the baby come out. When they asked, 'How did the baby get into mother's tummy?' we easily explained that mother and daddy together started the baby there–something like planting a seed together so it would grow into a beautiful baby. They also knew that when the new baby came, they would have to help around the house while mother was in the hospital. They were all excited when they would get to help tend the new baby."

Another characteristic of effective families is that some activities are reserved for the family, no questions asked. In other words, the parents give clear messages about the priority of family time. Children do not "own" all of their own hours. For example, many parents stress that attending church is a family activity, a value they enforce and reinforce even when one parent has to go early or stay late in meetings, and even when teenagers exasperate them by dawdling during preparation. They do not leave children home and they do not leave children to come on their own. As a result, they communicate two things: the value of church attendance and the value of family participation.

Even when the children, at their worst, are giving the most grudging of physical compliance, they are still learning these two values. Most of the time, of course, they are also hearing in talks and classes a repetition and reinforcement of the same values and goals their parents teach them at home.

One Idaho family had a delightful variation on this "always in church" rule. When their three oldest surviving children, spaced two years apart, decided to test the rule, the parents countered ingeniously: "We explained to them that they had their free agency about attending Church meetings. If they choose not to honor the Sabbath and consider it just another day, then they are free to stay home—and do a weekday chore that we assign. So far they have chosen to attend their meetings." A Salt Lake City family of eight, ages nine to twenty-seven, discussed how church attendance never became a problem: "The father has always just led by example and the children follow. The mother also is dedicated and attends without fanfare. Going to meetings is *just what our family does*". "All of our children have sometimes chosen to stay home from church, but they quickly recognize that they'd rather go." In a whimsical afterthought, the mother added, "We let them choose and, fortunately, they have always chosen well. I don't know what we'd do if they didn't."

SUPPORTING EACH OTHER

Our research showed that whenever a child or a parent takes part in church and community life outside the family circle, it is still considered a family affair. Everyone goes. Everyone is pleased about a family member giving a talk in church or being in a play or program. As children get older and participate in sports, dance, or music, everyone attends the games or recitals. One Utah couple with five children noted: "We attend all of the children's activities: dance, piano recitals, tennis matches, gymnastic meets. We have gone to horseback competitions together for twelve years."

When the parents cannot attend a child's event, they find other ways to communicate their support. One mother indicated how she handled the sheer logistics of not being able to be in two places at the same time: "We have a large family, and time does not permit us to go to everything we would like to. If we cannot attend a game in which our son is playing or a meeting where our daughter is speaking, we try to go out of our way to say something about it. For example, a comment like, 'Brother Briggs told me that you really gave a good talk,' helps the child know that we are interested and would have been there if we could have."

Children in such families have learned that the achievement of one family member reflects positively on all of them. There is no sense of competition but rather a sense of reinforcement—at least in theory. Most families agreed that they worked toward this feeling but had better success at some times than at others.

Family Courtesy

Most effective parents also establish and enforce standards of family courtesy. They do not expect automatic love from their children; they expect to teach it to them. One Utah family with seven children quoted 1 John 4:7 in part before every meal: "Let us love one another." At times, the tone of voice hardly matched the words, but the sheer repetition—three times a day, week after week, month after month, year after year—gradually sank in.

"We try to give a lot of emotional support to each child," said one set of parents. Another couple said, "We often tell each other we have the best family in the world. There are a lot of hugs and "I love you's." One Utah family even has a code word,, which they use to say "I love you."

Most parents feel that they should set an example by apologizing when necessary. "We think it is important that our children learn from their mistakes," said one couple. "Therefore we feel we must let them know we make mistakes too; and when we err, we try to admit it."

An Idaho couple carefully taught their ten children to

say "thank you," "please," "I'm sorry," and "I love you." The mother explained, "My husband and I speak to each other that way. It's a thrill to overhear them playing or working and saying, 'Please.' Even salespeople who regularly call on us have commented on the special feeling we have in our home."

Hardly any family would think of quarreling as positive. Most families have rules against it, but a certain amount of quarreling among children is inevitable, no matter how strenuously it is discouraged. How do these effective families deal with sibling squabbles?

Many of them have explicit rules about what is and is not acceptable behavior: no fighting, quarreling, or bickering. Parents intervene quickly when they hear voices begin to rise, sometimes to suppress the symptoms with a firm reminder of the rule, sometimes to send the combatants to different rooms, sometimes to talk through the differences and negotiate a compromise, and sometimes to say, "You can settle this disagreement by yourselves in a friendly way with no yelling. Come tell me when you've worked things out." One practical mother of seven always considers hunger and fatigue as possible causes of quarreling. Even if the disagreement is rooted in other causes, the offer of a snack or rest is sometimes enough to ward off an explosion.

One mother emphasized a principle that most of the families would probably agree with: "We spend *a lot* of time training our children when they're young. And we don't fight ourselves." Another mother observed that she and her husband consciously began praising positive interaction among the children when they noticed that "some of the other family members (our brothers and sisters) spend a good deal of time talking about how much their children fight. I don't think they fight any more than most families, but they keep focusing on it rather than on the good things that happen."

Several of the families reported, with real appreciation, the quality of love among their children. A delightful example came from one Utah family with nine: "The children not only love each other but they respect and enjoy each other. They enjoy talking for hours with each other. Older children work and play with the younger ones. Our seventeen-year-old son took the four-year-old twins along on one of his dates. He thought it was great, but his girlfriend may have been surprised." An eighteen-year-old boy, one of ten children, spent his summer vacation with his married sister in Connecticut, tending her four children.

TAKING CHARGE OF FAMILY TIME

Another common element in most of these effective families was a deliberate structuring of family time. In one family it is a rule: "Every family member is expected to eat and pray together at least two times daily."

One Utah couple with seven children deliberately plans their time around togetherness. In addition to showing up en masse for recitals, talks, games, baptisms, and ordinations, they "work in the yard together, pulling weeds in the garden in twos and threes or sevens. Mowing the lawn usually sees two working together—and talking. Canning fruit or drying apricots is a family project. Some do all of some jars, which they then enter in the county fair. Every member of the family has won ribbons and trophies which are displayed around the house."

This family also noted: "Although many of our projects are family projects, we also encourage all our children to achieve in some area. We try to plan activities and events that will focus attention for their successes just on them, so they can know the feeling of having family and friends know they have done well. Sometimes helping our boys earn their Eagle Scout rank has taken lots of parental effort. A good report card may require evening study time with the parent learning new things, helping, encouraging, and sometimes insisting. Although our family consumes a lot of popcorn together, it's hardly ever at the movies or in front of the television.

"We try to keep coordinated with a family calendar, filled in at family home evening for as far ahead as possible and quickly reviewed at the breakfast table for the day—after scripture reading but before toast. And occasionally we send out an emergency SOS to our home teacher to please pick up someone from somewhere because something unexpected came up."

One Texas family felt apologetic about not having family home evening every week and family scripture study every day but felt that "spending *good* time together" was one of their strengths as a family. In spite of busy work schedules, they made time to have family parties at home where everyone could invite guests. They went to the beach together, went crabbing together, and also went out to dinner together. A Utah family with seven children speculated, "Maybe we should be more 'others' oriented" but listed the traits that make their family special. "We like each other. We're friends as well as family. We enjoy each other's company, are interested in each other and our accomplishments, have a strong sense of loyalty, take pride in one another's achievements, and have fun together." One of the most important activities they do together is "just visiting together—having a lot of laughs."

Our research concluded that in effective families, vacations are given great importance. During these vacations, normal routines are suspended and parents and children can concentrate on enjoying each other in a pleasant setting. In fact, for many families, the time of the most family interaction is during the vacation. A significant number of families own or rent motor homes or campers to make traveling with a large group more convenient. One family has a fifteen-year tradition of "living in swimming suits for two weeks" at a beach house in California they rent from a family they know. The father gets only two weeks vacation in the summer and has willingly chosen to spend it in this way the major part of his married life. "It has become a family tradition, and everyone loves to go and to be together. We surf, swim, play ball, sunbathe, go out and play tennis or golf nearby, read, play games, eat, and just have a good time. Sometimes other relatives will stop by for a visit and everyone enjoys that. It seems that everyone gets along better on vacation than at any other time during the year. We always take along some old familiar games (Old Maid, Detective, Monopoly) and some new ones like Trivial Pursuit. All our children who have married still want to come back for the family vacation."

A Utah father with five children said: "Early on we discovered that one of the most unifying experiences for our family was to travel or take a family vacation. Since there were no others around to play with, the children had to relate to each other and to us, and we found that we really enjoyed each other and had fun together. These outings gave us memories that we will share and talk about all our lives. My wife and I adopted a slogan: 'Experiences are more important than things.' Often we were faced with a decision: Should we take a family trip or buy a new refrigerator or new carpet? Almost always, the trip won out."

TALKING

National studies on family interaction have become popular since about the mid-1960s, when the "generation gap" was discovered. Families, like other social organizations, are beginning to deal with "wellness," making plans and choices to maximize the potential of each family member. Wellness is becoming a more widespread goal of many families, and it is also being translated into programs and plans to help increase the chance of obtaining it. Open communications is one of the most important factors identified in family health so far.

The two hundred families in our study would probably agree on the importance of communication—and their family patterns bear out the value. Parents and children in these families talk a lot, and willingly spend the time to be with each other. One father put it this way: "I would say if there is one thing that has made a difference in our family, it has been that we have always talked together. When our children were little, they would all climb in our bed and we would talk. The kids loved to hear how we met and got married and all the events around their births and how special each one was. This pattern has continued through high school and college and even now that some are married. It is common to have these older children sit around the bed on the floor and talk until we have to kick them out so we can get some sleep."

Ninety-nine percent of the parents listed "talking" as their most crucial teaching method. Only "example" ranked higher at 100 percent. And when discipline was needed, "talking with" a child was seen as the most important method in 97 percent of the families.

When children do something of merit, 88 percent of the parents respond most frequently with verbal praise. In fact, almost any change in children's behavior in these families— good or bad—produces increased communication.

Effective fathers and mothers perceive themselves as spending a remarkably large amount of time talking with each child every day. We asked parents how often they engaged in the following activities:

1. Sit around talking together
   as a family   daily 68%   weekly 25%
2. Talk to each child   daily 81%   weekly 12%
3. Talk with children about
   their personal concerns daily 42%   weekly 41%

Parents also said that the father and mother spent, on the average, twenty-five minutes a day together talking *with* each child. Additionally, mothers claimed they averaged thirty-three minutes daily talking with each child, while fathers averaged about eighteen minutes. In families with six children, this could amount to three hours a day for husband and wife together, an extremely high figure, especially when the husband reportedly spends another two hours in private conversation with the children and the wife spends another three hours. If they are accurate in this perception, talking together has been made an extremely high priority. Almost certainly some parents included time spent talking as a group, because some of them specified mealtimes as conversational hours, when more than one child would be present. An interesting study would examine the parents' perception of time spent in group conversation with two or more children and compare it with their children's perceptions of the time their parents spent with them in both private and group conversation .

We asked parents, "Overall, who talks to the children most?" Sixty-eight percent said that the mother talked with the children most often. Out of all the families, only two (1 percent) said the father talked to the children most. Another 27 percent said that both parents talked to the children equally but at separate times.

One mother felt that the figures might not represent family interactions accurately and added, "I know I spend more time talking with the children than my husband does. But the children respect their father very much and look up to him as the spiritual head of our home. When he does talk to the children either alone or all together, they usually listen very carefully." Another mother also agreed that she spent more time talking to the children than her husband did, but when she boldly asked them, "Who's the boss?" they all agree their father is. "I am probably more aggressive and outspoken", she says, but they look to their dad for a final word." One couple saw this pattern as a result of personality: "Father is quieter and more reserved, but the children respect him and seek his counsel. They understand and respect his nature, but this may have been a problem for them at times, just as the mother's nature has been at times."

As with other activities that foster family unity, talking is a planned activity, arranged and encouraged even when it's inconvenient. "Our talking is mostly at bedtime or after every sensible person should be asleep," says one father wryly. In one Utah family, where two of the married children live out of state, weekly long-distance phone calls are part of the family budget.

One self-employed businessman routinely puts in long days and sometimes has to work weekends, but every week "he takes one child at a time with him to the office and takes him or her out to lunch. And he talks with them before they go to bed."

Several couples who articulate the value of spending time with each child have set up formal mechanisms to ensure it happens. One couple reports, "This means setting aside time with each child to talk, discuss, do something together, and help them learn in their own areas of interest." Monthly father-child interviews seem to be effective, and no one complained that they seemed stilted or unnatural. "I talk with each child about what has happened during the month, review any problems, give encouragement, and set goals," said one father. "I like being able to have time that I can't be 'squeezed out' of," said another. One set of Utah parents, whose seventh child is eighteen, wished the ideas of personal interviews with each child had been around when their children were younger. "We would have started it at a very young age," they said.

Several of the couples mentioned "monitoring" to catch problems early and then spending extra time with the troubled child. One couple said, "We try as much as possible to interact with each child and watch for special needs very carefully. The children interact with each other a great deal and will handle some situations themselves, but when they have special needs, they come to us." The parents of an Idaho family, who own a farm equipment business, consciously included their ten children in the family business. We "worked together and talked as we worked. If we noticed something amiss, we took time to be with that child alone."

At least two families have consciously taken advantage of contact times, turning them into conversation times. One Idaho couple commented, "The fact that our drapery business *is* in our home and we are close to schools is a special help. The kids come home one or two at a time, and Mom and Dad are both there to listen to the events of the day. We are do-it-yourselfers, and there are lots of talking opportunities as we work together. The kids work with their dad on the car and home upkeep and repair, and with Mom on cleaning, canning, and sewing. When we help the kids with their projects, we talk. Gathering for prayers night and morning usually winds up in a gab session unless we are under time pressures. After meals, we sometimes wind up visiting for an hour after we are through eating. Whenever a question arises, we look it up in one of our reference books and share it with the family. We save jokes to bring to the family or read each other sections of books we're reading, then talk about it."

A second set of parents observed, "Our most meaningful talks have been in the car, going to and from music lessons, ballgames, and so on, and also after children come home from dates and parties. It always pays to be waiting up to share in their joys or sorrows."

THE EXTENDED FAMILY

While popular literature might portray each family as somewhat isolated from any extended family network, studies done on families in Detroit in the 1960s show an active and healthy pattern of interaction among extended families. Mormon families are also plugged into family networks. For most of the effective families in this study, grandparents, aunts, uncles, and cousins are an important part of the family unit. Only five families, 2.5 percent, said they were "seldom" involved with the extended family. In some cases, long distances from other family members made visiting a rare occurrence, and several other families had *no* close living relatives. Out of the remaining families, 51 percent responded "always" to the following statement: "We are involved in family activities with our extended family." Forty-four percent answered this question "usually" or "sometimes," and the remainder did not answer the question.

Three-fourths of these families would "always" or "usually" attend family reunions. In contrast, a study in progress in western Canada and the Midwest shows that only 10 percent of their families attend reunions. Forty percent specifically mentioned that for vacations, they would visit relatives, either as the main purpose of a trip or as part of a trip. One couple explained that they tried to plan their vacations to include seeing a "new place," either a Church-history site like Winter Quarters, some natural feature like Yellowstone Park, or a site connected with national history like Mount Rushmore or Valley Forge.

A Utah family with nine children joins the extended family for a week's camping at Yellowstone, a tradition that has now lasted thirty-five years. When asked to list their three greatest strengths as a family, the first was love, the second was a sense of stewardship for talents, and the third was "being supported and valued by members of our extended family on both sides."

One Utah couple, the parents of ten children, only two of which are unmarried, writes a monthly letter summarizing events from their journals. Not only do the children get a copy but so do their brothers, sisters, and grandparents.

One family of four in Utah, in close proximity to relatives on both sides of the family, noted, "When more than a week goes by that we haven't seen grandparents, aunts, uncles, and cousins, our children begin to ask, 'When are we going to see Grandma and Grandpa?' or 'When are they coming to see us?' Thirty of us are generally together *at least* once a month and sometimes every week. We celebrate each birthday and anniversary, and we often get together for no special reason."

Possibly as a result of this kind of attention, relatives were most frequently listed as family heroes, after Spencer W. Kimball (president of the Church when the survey was first administered) and several other Church figures. Relatives as heroes easily outranked sports figures, popular entertainers, or politicians. One couple said, "We all follow

BYU sports and identify with various sports figures. But the children look up to their grandparents more than anyone else. They were strong, exceptional people. Even our married children talk about them and their ideals." Another couple with five married children said, "We admire a son-in-law who has had a lot of adversity."

The intergenerational impact of family members on family solidarity might make a rewarding study in itself. A family that can supply its own heroes communicates a sense of clan distinction that makes belonging to the family something to be proud of. Family heroes constantly reinforce for children the notions of "our family," "my grandparents," "my father," or "my cousin." One family who had a relative listed in *Who's Who in America* was very proud of this fact. She showed the entry to a lot of people, and reminded the children of it. It was not so much an individual accomplishment as it was a family achievement.

We didn't actually tabulate the number of times the phrase "spend time" appeared in the answers to the questionnaire. Our impression is that every set of parents used it at least three or four times. Its sheer repetitiveness impressed us. Parenthood is expensive—it costs time. We've heard a great deal about "quality time" in parenting in recent years, and certainly there's a great deal to be said for intelligent intervention and deliberately planned interaction. The two hundred families in our survey would probably be advocates of "quantity time" as well. They spent time working with their children, talking with their children, being with their children, and teaching their children.

On the whole, we would have to say that one of the reasons these families are so united, bound by commonly shared gospel values and intense love, is the sheer number of hours they have put into building high-quality relationships with each other. "No one else has a higher investment in these children," these parents seem to say, "and there's nothing else we value so much."

CHAPTER THREE

KEY 3

ESTABLISHING CLEAR FAMILY GOALS

Effective families can tell if they're making progress because they know where they're going. These parents articulate a clear vision of what they want for the whole family and for each family member—to be "together forever." Planning on forever, they are strongly motivated to maintain a high degree of unity and affection within the family. When inevitable adversities come, it is toward each other that they turn for support.

We asked parents, "What special goals do you have as a family?" We offered some choices, and here's how they responded:

Have children serve missions	100%
Have children marry in the temple	100%
Have children get good education	99%
Develop a strong sense of family unity	98%
Help each child to develop a strong feeling of self-worth or a good self-concept	98%
Have every family member active in the Church	99%

Then we specifically invited them to, "list other important goals that you have as a family." That list included:

Being good Christians and good citizens	37%
Putting the family first	22%
Business success	16%
Grades	10%
Health	2%
Sports	1%

It comes as no surprise that the parents wanted their children to be active in the Church, go on missions, and marry in the temple. We discuss their support of public education in Chapter five and how they developed family unity in Chapter three. This chapter concentrates on parents' feelings about developing self-esteem in their children and on the individual goals that each couple sets for their own family.

DEVELOPING SELF-ESTEEM IN CHILDREN

A wide range of studies has shown the importance of children's feelings of self-worth as an influence in their decisions and actions. Those who have a poor self concept are more likely to engage in self-defeating behaviors. Research in this area also shows that children's self concept is learned, particularly as they hear others talk about them or compare them to others in either positive or negative terms. Since comparisons are most often made with other family members, friends, or relatives, the influence of these people on children's self-worth is vital.

On the chart we asked for demographic data (like age and sex) for each individual in the family, we also asked parents to evaluate "each person's feelings of self-worth "1-High, 2-Medium, 3-Low." We assumed that there would be an implied comparison with others that they knew. Here are the ratings:

	Husbands' Self-Esteem	Wifes' Self-Esteem
High	73%	64%
Medium	23%	33%
Low	3%	2%

In reporting results for the children, parents rated 75 percent of them with high feelings of self-worth, 20 to 25 percent with medium, and only 1 to 2 percent with low. The only real variation from this pattern was that the third child generally rated lower: 53 percent have high self-esteem and 46 percent have medium. (We found nothing in birth-order research that might provide a reason for this.)

None of these results is surprising. Positive people come out of positive environments and, in turn, reinforce positive feelings for each other. When couples added comments to the self-esteem section of the survey, they usually described a problem. One couple explained that one of their children had low self-esteem from babyhood, and that being consistently positive and nurturing had been a great challenge for them. Another couple, the wife of which rated her feelings of self-worth as low and her husband's as medium, had four children who also rated either medium or low. "We tried," they commented briefly.

A Utah mother with seven children listed as an adversity "one child with low self-esteem from birth." She commented, "It was long and slow to work out but has been done, I'm grateful to say. We handled it with much talk and love and patience, and talk and patience and love, and then still more."

A Utah mother rated her seven children and herself high in self-esteem. She explained that one of the important factors in making their family strong was "building high self-esteem through a positive, nurturing, loving attitude toward the children, encouraging them to choose the right and showing them what right is, and manifesting a commitment to the marriage, the family, and the Church." A California mother with three sons jotted down by the question on self-worth: "If we can accomplish this one, then all the others will be easier."

An Idaho couple with three children rated everyone in the family as having medium self-worth. The mother noted, next to the goal of helping each child develop self-worth, "This is the hardest to do." One Salt Lake City mother with ten adopted children described their greatest challenge as a couple: "Helping the children have a good self image and not always succeeding." Then she articulated their family philosophy: "We know that we are here to help one another. Knowing that we are an eternal family also tells us that we must work out our problems and difficulties. We keep telling our children that we are experiencing the *adventure* of our lives—this life on earth—and to accept it as such. When you're down, don't stay down, because there's always something around the corner. And most importantly, we teach our children that everyone is here to learn and that some have progressed more than others. Everyone must be accepted for the level they are on, but do not allow whatever level they are on to affect you and how you act. Love God and serve and keep your testimony in spite of bad experiences. Have a good sense of humor. Go for it!"

WHAT EFFECTIVE FAMILIES WANT

About 25 percent of the couples did not add any additional goals to the checklist we provided, but this section made some of the most interesting reading in the entire questionnaire. Some of the questions we used in follow-up interviews originated from this section. Many of the goals were related to topics already discussed, such as maintaining strong unity. Some typical goals are "taking care of each other in need," "maintaining strong family ties after the children leave home," "staying close as a family and as an extended family," "continuing the close-knit family unity in generations to come—with my husband and me still at the head of our extended family, worthy and qualified to give counsel and advice," "rendering assistance to the children's grandparents and other older people," "having the family love and enjoy one another," "doing things together and including the extended family," and "participating in activities together." Several couples mentioned attendance at family reunions as a goal, and one couple with four children, two of them married, described a "family cruise" as a goal.

GOSPEL-RELATED GOALS

Many couples mentioned goals like "becoming a celestial family," "attaining the celestial kingdom," "gaining eternal life," and "being together eternally." A Utah couple with nine children wrote, "Our biggest goal is to learn to listen and understand and *follow* the promptings that come to us from the Holy Ghost." This is the same couple who consciously taught their children to pray and listen for the guidance of the Holy Ghost from babyhood and who, when the children needed discipline, asked them to pray and listen to the Spirit. All five married children of this couple were married in the temple, and all mission-age sons have served missions.

A Texas couple in their fifties, with four daughters, the youngest being twenty and a stake missionary, has a goal of going on a mission themselves. A Utah couple has as a goal "internalizing the principles of the gospel." A California couple lists as a family goal, "to be strong Christians and serve the Lord all our lives." An Idaho couple with six daughters "would like each of our girls to be happily married and have a good family; and we'd like all of us to be together in the celestial kingdom." Two of their daughters are married—one with one child and the other with four, and a third daughter is divorced. An Idaho couple with five living children, with only the oldest married, want their children to "marry and raise a good strong family and be better people than their parents." An Idaho farmer with twenty-one children by four marriages lists as goals for his children: "Always support Church authorities, always have and use a temple recommend, and maintain individual integrity," along with "being financially independent." An Idaho couple with seven children wants, "happiness for each member." One Salt Lake City couple with five children, four married with eight children among them, reflected their delight in family life by listing as a goal, "seeing the children with families of their own." A Wyoming couple with three children, none of whom are married yet, has "happy marriages" as a major goal.

One Wyoming couple had two sons who were killed at ages nine and seven. For them, an important goal is "to be a celestial family and be with the two that have gone on ahead of us." A Utah couple with seven children, six living, wrote "enduring to the end" as a family goal. A Salt Lake City couple with two sons and three daughters wrote they wanted their children to "keep a proper perspective on what is really worthwhile in life—who you are and not how much you have."

EDUCATIONAL AND ECONOMIC GOALS

Financial stability and security appeared as a goal for a significant number of couples. A Salt Lake City couple with six children, all of whom are college graduates except for a son who is a college junior, wrote that a family goal is to "help each one get started in their own homes, businesses, and so on." A Texas couple with five temple married daughters and one son waiting for his mission call wanted their children to "be self-reliant and dependable." A Provo professor and his wife, with six children–three sons and three daughters–listed as an important goal, "becoming good providers and being financially sound." For one Idaho family of seven, the goal is to "have each child be able to function as a mature, responsible, independent person as early as possible."

A Montana farm couple wants their eight children to "have a good business and be able to live comfortably." An Idaho couple (the husband of which is a travel agent, the wife a teacher) wants their four children, ages eighteen to twenty-six, to "succeed in their professions." The California parents of seven children say that "to be ambitious" is one of their family rules. A Utah couple with eight children at two-year intervals, lists "financial management" and "helping others" as family goals.

Other goals are "have each person prepared for an occupation," "make the farm pay," "live within our means," "be financially secure," "have a satisfactory profession that suits abilities and interests," "learn the importance of work," "achieve economic independence," "have independence from parents," "be out of debt," "learn the work ethic," and "have strong career goals."

Some of the professional goals are broad enough to include more general self-development and educational goals. A Provo family with seven children with the father and oldest son both occupied as college professors, lists as goals, "Discovering and developing talents. Developing a love for truth and learning." An Idaho farm family with seven children wants each "to develop their talents and interests." A Utah couple with seven children said they "expect each to find his or her special talent or interest and excel in it. Finances are not a high goal, nor is competitiveness." All of their children are making above-average grades in school; one is in medical school and another is a music student at the college level. One Wyoming couple with seven children said that an important goal for their family was, "Don't interfere with private time. Let each child choose to enjoy his or her special interests." A Salt Lake City couple with five daughters and a son has set the goal of developing musical and athletic talents. For a Wyoming family with seven living children–four daughters and three sons–Eagle Scout awards for the boys and the honor roll for everyone were high expectations. For a Provo family, a strong goal was "to acquire culture and an appreciation of the arts."

RELATIONSHIP GOALS

Many couples mentioned the importance of communication and related skills as family goals. Others listed the kinds of qualities that would foster good relationships for their children. An Idaho family with ten children works hard "to teach the children manners and behavior that will help them be welcomed wherever they may go." "We especially teach them to be appreciative of the things others do for them (especially of their Father in Heaven for his blessings) and to express thanks easily." An Idaho couple with three children lists as a family goal, "Be sensitive to and care for other people." A Utah couple with nine children has a goal of, "improving love at home." A Utah couple with two sons and three daughters, all married except for one daughter who is engaged, wrote that a goal is "keeping lines of communication open among family members and in our own individual families."

For a Utah couple with eight unmarried children ranging in age from two to twenty-one, "respect for others" is a family goal. An Idaho couple with seven children listed "having a sense of humor." A Utah mother of three listed "have fun as a family." An Idaho couple with seven children listed "cheerfulness" as a family priority. A Montana blended family valued "honesty and communication." Another family wanted their children to "learn to reverence all of God's creations, recognize the right of all to their opinions, and learn the absolute necessity of being kind."

SERVICE GOALS

Many couples listed "service," "being good citizens," "patriotism," "loyalty to country with a knowledge of correct economic and political principles upon which the nation was founded," and being "responsible members of the community" among their important family goals. A Utah couple with eight sons and a daughter have seen all of the boys except their sixteen-year-old serve missions and six marriages performed in the temple. One of their important family goals was to "be useful citizens and neighbors, helping others with their means, time, and talents." A Utah couple with seven children said: "We want our children to be responsible workers and serve the community. We think it is important to plant more than we harvest, to help others less fortunate." One Texas couple (the husband of which is a physician and the mother is an artist) wrote as a family goal, "Be an asset to the community."

Goals are not always accomplished as parents would like. Many of the parents pointed out that despite their best efforts, sometimes a child, or maybe two, drifted away from the plan of the family. Parents were aware if they had made mistakes in implementing their plans. Sometimes they felt they were too strict, or maybe not strict enough. At times they might have given too much to one child and not enough to another. The children made mistakes, and the parents did not always know exactly how to respond. One Montana mother probably spoke for many parents when she looked at her five mission-age sons, only one of whom filled a mission, and confessed that "some hopes went down the tubes."

Despite certain weaknesses and some failures, however, these parents have a vision of where they wanted to go and some understanding of what they need to do to get there. Many of the families seem to evaluate their progress continually, like the couple who talked together to assess how they were doing as parents and how well their children seemed to be doing. As they sensed the need for new directions in some areas, they might have held a family discussion, perhaps a family home evening, where the family planned to correct their course. At times this correction may have involved the entire family; at other times, it might have been directed toward one person who was struggling.

Successful parents seem to know the state of the family. They see their goals and their progress and sort of tap things back into shape periodically. The knowledge of where they are and what is needed requires husbands and wives who understand one another and want to get the job done. In contrast, one of the less-effective mothers confessed, "I don't know, but we're just at the stage where we have several teenagers, and they're acting just about like we did when we were younger. We've attempted to fix the problems , but it never works as well as we hope it will. I guess we'll just live with it and maybe the kids will shape up when they get married. That's our only hope, I guess."

In sharp contrast—not in satisfaction but in commitment—is the comment of one Salt Lake City mother of eight children, seven of whom are living. She wrote that one of their most important family goals is "to have joy" then added a candid progress report: "I think we will not know if we have raised a successful family until we see how our grandkids turn out. Also, I must admit I think we would not have had as much success as we have if we had insisted on following every Church plan to perfection. We cannot really separate out family and the Church, but in some instances, our family has had first priority when it came to choosing how we would spend our time. Our children all know the Church is first in our lives—without them having to be second. We are not a perfect family. We have a long way to go, but we are all on the way. For this we are grateful yet humbled by our shortcomings. We want to be better. We will be! Twenty years from now, if we are identified as a successful family, it will be more believable. Right now, we think it is premature."

Key 4

Using Discipline in the Family

None of the highly effective couples in our survey would say that their family is perfect. As one mother said, "We find there are problems in every phase of our lives. We just get through one set and find another. It is literally [true] that the ultimate test of a 'good' family is to be able to endure to the end."

However it is also true that, at least during the time that the survey was conducted, other people felt that these parents were doing an effective job of rearing their children.

How do these parents get their children to do what they want them to? Do they have strict rules? Do they demand obedience to rules? Do they check on and control their children closely? The answer to all of these questions is "no." One of the patterns that stands out for almost every family is that they have a few, but specific, rules for their children. Even more important than the rules, however, are the expectations— they are high, they are clear, and they have a profound influence on the behavior of the children.

Expectations are a major part of what constitutes the

"culture" of family. They represent a general set of unofficial guidelines and standards that everyone in the family understands and accepts, though few families could give you a comprehensive list. As one teenager said: "I remember when one of my friends was over to our house on a Saturday night and asked if I would like to go to a movie with him on Sunday afternoon. Of course I said 'no', and he wanted to know why. He asked me if that was one of our rules. As I thought about it, it suddenly dawned on me that it was one of our rules except that no one had ever told me the rule, that I could remember. There are just a lot of things that our family does different from some others I know, but we just have come to expect the differences and think that is the best way to do things."

Another teenager in a highly effective family told of going home with a friend and showing his father his straight-A report card. The father smiled, gave his son a pat on the shoulder, and said, "Good job, son. I'm proud of you." The friend was dumbfounded. Later he told the son, "Your dad saw all those A's and told you that you had done a good job. I took my card to our dad and it was A's and B's and he was so delighted that he let me put my own phone in my room."

The son with the straight A's came from a family where good grades were expected. All of the children were expected to go to school every day, do all of their homework, and get grades consistent with their abilities. This son had always received straight A's and it was routinely expected that he would continue to do so.

In the survey, we asked each family some questions about rules, discipline, and motivation:

1. How many rules do you have for your children?

2. List what you consider to be the most important rules you have as a family.

3. How do you discipline your children? (We offered the choices of positive reinforcement, spanking, grounding, withdrawal of privileges, scolding, talking with them, giving them a "talking to," and "other." We also asked them to rank these discipline measures by how important they were in the family.)

4. How do the children generally respond to your discipline attempts?

5. For what kinds of things do you apply discipline?

6. How strict is your family compared with other families that you know?

7. Do you reward your children for some things? If yes, what rewards do you use? (We offered the choices of money, trips, TV time, praise, permission to do favorite activities, and "other.")

8. Which of these rewards has produced the best results for you?

9. What kinds of behavior do you give rewards for? (We offered the choices of practicing music lessons, giving talks, getting good grades, going to church, doing non-routine work, and "other.")

10. What are the things that your children *must* do? (We offered the choices of going to meetings, helping around the house, going to school every day, obeying Church standards, living the Word of Wisdom, taking part in family prayer, saving for missions, practicing music lessons, and "other.")

HOW MANY RULES?

Nearly 50 percent of the families indicated they had from zero to five rules. Thirty-one percent said they had between six and ten rules. This means that 80 percent of these families felt they had fewer than ten rules. Several families commented that they had many important and high expectations in the family but almost no rules, indicating that a rule represented something more formal than expectations. One Utah couple with five children did not give a number and said, "Our 'rules' are habit and are not itemized." In contrast, another Utah couple gave up counting and said, "We have more than twenty. They must be well understood for a large family to function and feel comfortable in their roles." Another family conveyed the same frustration with the assignment by quipping, "We've never really counted our rules. They so quickly become habits which become ways of life!"

Often rules were written down, usually discussed and identified as "one of the rules in our family." Whether written down or not, all family members generally understood what constitutes a family rule.

One of the most interesting findings came, however, when we asked parents to identify their three most important rules. The three most common rules were:

1. *Every member of the family must be treated with respect.* Over 60 percent of the families had this rule. No verbal or physical abuse is allowed, no name calling or hurtful comments, and no fighting. An especially serious violation of the rule was to talk back to the parents, and especially to the mother. Few children ever dared talk back

to their father, and usually it was the father who insisted the children be respectful to their mother. One Wyoming ranching couple with six children reported: "We have this rule: 'Thou shalt not hassle thy Mother. Period.' Dad's rule number one." A related aspect was "good language," and some families resorted to the old but effective "washing out the mouth with soap" penalty for infractions.

2. Family members must tell the parents where they are going and when they will be back.

Fifty-four percent of the families had this rule. Although this rule tended to relax as the children got older, a surprising number of the parents who mentioned it had curfews or check-in times for all children living at home, whatever the age. A variation is the rule of a Washington family, with four children, that "no matter what, we get a phone call if they're going to be later than they'd planned." Another family had no set curfew, but the children were required to wake up the parents when they returned.

Some families indicated that this rule became something of a sore spot between parents and older children, particularly when these children (especially boys) came home from missions. The returned missionaries often wanted to be allowed to come and go from the home at will, while the parents still wanted to know where they were going and when they would be back. That had always been the rule, and the parents wanted the rule to still be in force. However, the sons now felt that they were adults and the rules should no longer apply. Families apparently need some rules for the home to operate in an effective manner and the rules have to include all who live there—whatever the age.

By requiring to know the whereabouts of the children,

parents are in effect saying to them, "We love you and want to know that you will be all right." This requirement also implies that the child will not be in the wrong place and doing the wrong thing. One mother had a rule that the children must come in after dates and kiss her good night before they went to bed. Not only could she be sure that they were home safe, but it gave her a chance to talk about anything really important that had happened. Also, she noted, "I think that the children were not tempted with Word of Wisdom problems because they knew that when they kissed me goodnight, I would be in a pretty good position to smell any deviation."

3. *Our family behaves with integrity, especially dependability and honesty.*

Nearly 50 percent of the families had some form of this rule. Many parents said that they explained it to their children in this way: "If you accept an assignment, you should be dependable and fulfill it." "If people are counting on you, you must fulfill whatever obligation it is, even if you don't enjoy it." "You are expected to be honest—to tell the truth, to not lie, cheat, or steal." Many families reported at least one incident of a child stealing something at an early age. The parents would insist that the child make it right. "Each one of our children has taken something from a store when they were young," said one Idaho couple with ten children. "We took each one back, had them apologize to the store owner, and had them work to pay it off. We've never had to do this more than once for any child." Church activity, with assignments to give a talk, attend a meeting, or accept an assignment, came under this dependability rule as well.

These families were large, busy, and hard working. The

parents clearly needed some assurance that their children would be where they said they'd be and do what they said they'd do. One farm couple explained, "If we left the kids with the milking, we just assumed that it would get done. The milking has to be done, and there is no room for any kind of excuse. They know that if they are detained somewhere for some important reason, they had better get in touch with some of the neighbors and have them start the milking."

Several parents also had firm rules about the use of private property. Some said that if one child used another person's belongings without asking permission, the matter would be discussed in family council and a penalty decided there.

In addition to these three rules, shared by more than half of the families, another cluster of three rules are shared by about 25 percent. First is the rule that each child must do his or her share of the work. Some families write out weekly lists of chores each person is to do, while other families simply have "understood" assignments. Many farm families, for instance, tend to assign more outside chores to the sons, while daughters concentrate on helping their mother with household tasks. Other families assigned chores more or less by age, with one child inheriting a task from an older sibling when he or she became old enough to do it. Still other parents simply assign the children jobs on the basis of whatever needs to be done. They frequently remind them, "Remember, everyone is supposed to do his or her fair share."

Teaching children to work, assigning work fairly within the home, and launching children into the larger world of work is certainly too complicated to be dispatched by a couple of rules. Chapter seven discusses this method in greater detail.

A second rule shared by 25 percent of the families was the requirement to treat the home with respect. This usually meant that children were not to break things, "roughhouse," or be careless with property that would be expensive to replace or that had sentimental value. One rebellious teenager deliberately flouted this rule by making greasy footprints on the carpet.

The third rule, which about 25 percent of the families said they had made explicit for their children, was living Church standards. This rule covered a multitude of activities: not dating until sixteen, participating in family prayer and family home evening, not swearing, paying tithing, and reading the scriptures. A Utah Valley couple with six children observed dryly, "It is a rule to obey the rules." However, all of the families indicated in one way or another that adherence to Church standards was an expectation more fundamental and pervasive than a rule.

DISCIPLINE

Of course, children sometimes break rules, and parents must then decide what to do. From a long-term perspective, a rule serves a function even if a child persists in defying it. A child who knows that the family standard forbids smoking may experiment with smoking during the growing-up years, but the clear standard of right and wrong is there. He uses that rule as a measure of his own conduct, and it generally serves as a constraint and eventually as a motivation in helping him change.

When we asked parents to identify the disciplinary measures they used with their children, this was the resulting order:

1. *Positive reinforcement.* Eight-five percent of the parents listed this method as their first or second choice. Most of them felt that by identifying the behavior they wanted and praising the child for it, they reduced the probability of later bad behavior which they would then have to punish or try to correct. One set of parents observed, "When we tell our son how well he is doing, he just beams all over, and we know that he will work hard to do that same thing in the future. He really runs on praise. As parents, we can sure tell you that it is a lot more fun to praise than spank."

2. *Talking with the child.* A calm discussion of right and wrong was listed by 97 percent of the parents. One father wrote: "I try to teach my children correct principles so they can see what is right and wrong behavior, and hopefully they will be able to govern themselves. When one does something we feel is wrong I try to sit down with the child and ask the child if he or she understands why I am upset and why we are having this talk. I then try to get the child to see why it was wrong and to get him or her to agree to improve in the future."

3. *Withdrawing privileges.* Sixty-six percent of the parents used withdrawal of privileges, such as not being able to watch a favorite television program, go to a friend's house, or stay up late for a special event.

4. *Giving the child a "talking to."* Forty-five percent use this method of discipline. It would be interesting to know if

children make a distinction between "talking with" and "being talked to," but most parents did. In the second instance, more intense emotions are involved, there is less concern about having a discussion, and more emphasis on the parent talking. One child described it as "laying down the law."

5. *Grounding.* Forty-eight percent of the parents said that for serious disobedience by older children and teenagers, they withdraw permission for the child to date, visit friends, or use the car. Children are forbidden to leave the home except for school and necessary meetings for a certain period of time.

6. *Scolding.* In this scale of disciplinary measures, parents seemed to see scolding as the angriest form of communication they had with their children. Yelling threats, perhaps name-calling occurred, and many parents indicated that they lost their tempers. Some admitted saying things they later regretted. Only 55 percent said they used scolding while 45 percent said they did not. One father told us, "I scold the children at times, but mostly it grows out of my own frustration. If things aren't going well for my wife and me, we sometimes take it out on the kids. Sometimes they deserve it, though."

7. *Spanking.* This was the only form of physical punishment of suggested disciplines, and it was the last measure listed—by a rather wide margin. Forty-five percent of these parents, many of whose children had been small during a much less permissive period of child-rearing, said they had never spanked. Only 3 percent of the families indicated that spanking is their first discipline measure, and 9 percent list it as the second most important measure for them. Many families noted that spanking was age-

specific, that they stopped spanking at about age five to eight years. One family specified that they would spank until about age twelve. No one explicitly said that they spanked teenagers.

Still, in evaluating the highly controversial measure of spanking, it is interesting that 12 percent of these highly effective families see spanking as either first or second in importance in disciplining their children. These children seem to have turned out to be successful and effective, so it follows that spanking does not seem to have been disruptive and alienating. Perhaps that is because of the way it was done. One father described his spanking sessions this way: "I spanked my little children seldom, but it was serious. I would use a belt and it hurt. I also don't think I ever spanked any of my children as they got close to being a teenager. After a child had received a spanking, I think I honestly tried to follow the scriptural admonition to 'show forth afterwards an increase of love.' I would hold the child in my lap and hug and kiss him or her and tell that child I loved him or her. Then I would talk with that child about why I had given the spanking, and we would try to come to an agreement about avoiding problems in the future."

One of the fathers in our sample recalled something of his own growing-up years and remembers being spanked: "I got spanked a lot—more than I [spank] my own children. You know, the interesting thing about it is that I can never remember my dad spanking me when I was not at fault. Oh, I didn't like it at all, but even at that time I knew I had it coming. Now that I am older I can really say that all of the spankings did me good. We don't spank that much, though. Probably my wife has had more influence on better discipline than I."

Some parents use spanking as a last resort, when everything else seems to be ineffective. One son said about a spanking from his father: "Dad didn't spank any of us children very often, but when he did, we knew it was about something Dad felt very strongly about. It didn't take us kids long to learn what would get us a licking from Dad!" Still other parents used it on a serious first offense, particularly with little children, to emphasize the importance of obedience.

It would be interesting to probe the issue of spanking a little more. Would some parents, who would not spank a child on the bottom, *slap* their child? How do the children understand spankings? And how, for that matter, do the children perceive their parents' measures? Are they as aware of positive reinforcement as they are of grounding or spankings?

Still, the data from this research is clear. Almost all of the parents tried to control their anger when disciplining children and avoided the most emotionally intense forms of scoldings and spankings. Instead, they seem to use preventative discipline, first by teaching correct behavior and reinforcing it, then by using an escalating scale of communicating with the child—discussing, withdrawal of privileges, and so on. "And sometimes," sighed the parents of nine ranging from ages five to twenty-one, "you try everything and nothing works. Sometimes success is just a matter of the right combination of the child, the day, and the situation."

Many parents who added "other" forms of discipline agreed with the Utah parents of eight who listed "natural and logical consequences." Another frequently applied form of discipline was sending the offending children to their rooms. Some Utah parents of six found that waiting up for late teenagers was very effective because "they hated it." Some Wyoming parents of five children would use additional chores as a deterrent from disobedience. Another family found that "reasoning together" was their most effective method of discipline.

REASONS FOR DISCIPLINING

When we asked parents to identify the times they apply discipline, they gave these answers, listed in order of how frequently they occurred:

1. The child disobeys the parent's direct instructions to do or not do something, or violates one of the family's rules, expectations, or norms.
2. The child comes in later than agreed.
3. The child fights with siblings.
4. The child does not do assigned work.
5. The child treats parents or other family members with disrespect.

There is considerable overlap among these reasons. Most families would agree that doing assigned chores and not fighting are family *rules*, but obviously, obedience and responsibility are high *values* in all of these families. One parent said, "I feel that children should 'honor their father and mother,' and when they do not obey our requests I feel this is not honoring us." Many couples listed specific infractions that had triggered a discipline "clamp-down" like sassing, stealing, and jumping on the beds. One couple said they punished their thirteen-year-old for unauthorized joy-riding in the family car.

In an area so value-laden as discipline, and one for which advice from child-rearing experts has changed so conspicuously and quickly, many parents sometimes flounder and feel confused. In an interview, parents in one of the less-effective families mused, "If we could start over again, we would make up more rules. The kids have always done what they wanted to, and we thought that they would make the best choices, but they didn't, and now it is too late. Of course, we haven't done so well with the choices we made either." A father in another less-effective family stated, "My dad used a belt on me, and I think I turned out okay. It's the kids who don't get belted that end up in reform schools. They just run wild, and the parents don't line them up." A mother in another less-effective family commented somewhat wistfully, "Our standards are too high, I think. With our oldest children we get after them for not getting all A's on their report card. We never do tell them that they are doing well, even when they get better grades than most of their friends." Still another set of less-effective parents was completely frank about their motives in discipline: "We send them to their room a lot, and that gets them out of our hair and away from each other."

The highly effective families in our study were not immune from confusion and fatigue, but they seem to have thought through some of the issues more thoroughly and carefully. They also seem to have behaved more consistently. Many of them wrote illuminating comments about their philosophy of discipline. A Texas mother of four wrote: "When they were too small to reason with, we sometimes used spanking, but generally only when they were endangering themselves or someone else. When our oldest was about seven years old, a neighbor asked me how often I spanked him. I honestly couldn't recall the last time I'd had to spank him! In general, we have found that Joseph Smith's method worked best for us: Teach them correct principles and they govern themselves.

"I think the three oldest were probably all in grade school when we had a family council where they helped make the family rules and also determined what the punishments would be for breaking them. The rules included such things as (1) Be on time for dinner, (2) Let Mom or Dad know where you are going, (3) Bed made before school, and so on. They chose the penalties, and often they were more severe than we would have imposed. During the council meeting, we sometimes had to temper the penalties a bit. We didn't want penalties we weren't willing to enforce!

"We tried to help the children choose natural consequences. For example, the penalty for not making one's bed was to have to sleep on the floor the following night. The penalty for not checking out with Mom or Dad was being grounded for a period of time. Being late for dinner meant no dinner. The interesting thing about this whole plan was that they imposed punishment and really helped us enforce it with each other. When we might have been tempted to 'go soft' on one of them, the pressure from the others wouldn't allow it. 'Ha, ha, you sleep on the floor tonight!' was usually met with good-natured embarrassment. The first night of floor sleeping may have been fun, but it soon wore off.

"We asked our daughter about this method of discipline

the other day, and her comment was, 'We just knew if we didn't do right, you'd be so *disappointed* in us, and we didn't want that.'"

"Not all children would respond to this method in the way ours have, and perhaps we have not really been tested as parents. My grandmother used to say she wouldn't know what kind of parent she had been until she saw how her grandchildren turned out. She was training not only children but the next generation of parents! Too few young couples set out on the sea of matrimony with so large a view of their destination."

"In our family," echoed one set of Idaho parents with four children, "we did not use discipline so much as we allowed children to suffer the consequences of their own actions, without too much interference. If they stayed out late, they still had to get up early and go to work."

Another couple wrote, "We have felt it important that our children learn to complete assignments at an acceptable level. We try to follow up on every assignment to see if it was done and how it was done." Such consistency requires a high level of self-discipline in parents.

One Texas couple wrote, "Always resolve contention immediately." "We never let a child go to his or her room angry and let pouting make the problem larger." This couple also felt strongly that children shouldn't be "bribed for good behavior." Instead of offering rewards for good behavior, they tried to create an atmosphere with an "abundance of love where all the children could express their feelings, even angry ones, knowing that we loved and accepted them. We tried to have reasonable expectations but then tried to be absolutely consistent. Needless to say, we weren't always great at the consistency part." When their children pointed to other children who were rewarded for good behavior, these parents explained the principle behind their action: "In this life, rewards don't always come to deserving people. We need to learn to do right because it's right, not for any other reason. Only our Father in Heaven will always reward us. Trust him."

These parents used physical punishment to teach acceptable behavior at a very young age. If a child threw a tantrum in public, an immediate spanking in public followed. If one daughter bit another, the mother bit back, explaining that the daughter needed to know how it hurt. She then cuddled her until she was comforted and asking her if she understood about making a different choice the next time. The parents decided that at about the age of eight months, their children were old enough to be quiet in church. Each child got a "bare-bottomed spanking" for misbehaving, followed by explanation and loving. "With five of the children, it took only one experience. With one it took two. And with one it took five," the mother recalled. "All of our discipline is based on 'reproving betimes with sharpness'—perhaps not always moved upon by the Holy Ghost—then showing forth afterwards an increase of love, explaining, talking, and loving."

The mother wrote that as a result of this early and thorough training, "I could take our children anywhere and be proud. We called them our angels while we heard other parents referring to theirs as monsters and beasts. It's true that some of those children seemed hyper, rowdy, and snoopy. Perhaps because our expectations were clear and our discipline was consistent, we knew we could depend on ours." Furthermore, she said, "our girls have been such a good example for our [three younger] boys that we've never had any trouble with them."

Some parents focus on making the discipline itself a learning experience. "When we discipline, we ask our children to pray about the situation and listen to what the Holy Spirit tells them to do," wrote the Utah parents of nine. "Thus they are disciplined by a higher source than us, and by themselves." In answer to a question later in the survey about the three most important rules, the mother wrote, "Follow the Spirit! Follow the Spirit! Follow the Spirit. The children can always recognize it, for it encourages them to do good and gives them a joyous, peaceful feeling."

Another family reinforced agency by letting the children choose between two punishments or to choose their own. A Utah couple with seven children, ranging in age from five to twenty, checked all the forms of discipline except spanking as "number one" and explained, "The most important thing is that they know the price of their unacceptable behavior before the transgression. Then the form is really irrelevant." Still another set of Utah parents explained, "We have a high degree of trust that our eight children will make the right choices. We are generally tolerant of errors and treat them as errors rather than as a sign of badness".

One mother reflected ruefully, "We have not been strong disciplinarians. We didn't know how to be. But I was against hitting or spanking." In another family, the couple decided before they were married, "Our children will never own a car of their own until after marriage or mission. They would be privileged to use the family car when necessary and as they deserved to do so. We have never had a problem with discipline and cars with any of our nine children. We attribute this to making our decision and sticking to it."

Most parents probably agree about the importance of consistency. "We feel it is very important for parents to stick together on discipline whether they agree at the time or not." Another set of parents corroborated, "By being firm and not changing the discipline, we grew closer together." In a Utah family with seven children, the parents saw their discipline styles as very different. The mother did most of the discipline, using positive reinforcement and talking, and "not making an issue" out of rebellion but instead finding "another way to give the children the responsibility for their actions." The father was more strict about most things and tended to begin discipline with a "talking to." Both agreed, however, that they were more relaxed parents with the younger four than with the older three, and the wife felt good about supporting the father's discipline, even when she didn't agree with it.

Consistency did not necessarily mean doing things the same way all of the time. Several parents acknowledged the differences among their children: "Some of our children were very sensitive to heart-to-heart talks," said one mother. "Others sometimes required a loss of privileges to get their attention." Another couple observed that "our oldest often shuts us out. The other two are very attentive and have shown no signs of rebellion." In one Idaho family the father had been married four times. His first three wives died, leaving several small children each, and his fourth wife brought eight children of her own to the marriage. These parents had a firm rule of "never comparing children or what they do or do not do."

One couple wrote: "Our children have all been different from one another in many ways. A couple of them didn't seem to respond to discussions, and we had to spank them occasionally. Others we would talk to and they would just seem to understand and be willing to do what was right. One son would become very difficult and obstinate unless we found something to praise him for. A little good, honest praise would make him work all the harder to make sure that he would get praised again. As he grew older, we didn't have to praise him so much. He just got better in all areas, it seemed. We think we would praise more and spank much less if we were starting all over again."

The parents also revealed their own efforts at self-discipline in dealing with their children. "We always endeavor to be fair," said one couple. "We feel it is important to listen to them to know where they are coming from." Their commitment to listen defused anger and curtailed "explosive" disciplines. Another couple also set controls for themselves: "We tried not to discipline in front of other people. We learned early that if the kids were humiliated, even the best form of discipline would be ineffective." One father said, "I would spank only occasionally, and then I'd send them to find a stick while I collected my thoughts and feelings and evaluated them."

CHILDREN'S RESPONSE TO DISCIPLINE

In an attempt to determine effectiveness, we asked parents, "How do your children generally respond to your discipline attempts?" Three-fourths (76 percent) said that their children generally accepted it. One couple said that "closer relationships and mutual respect" resulted from their discipline. An older couple, the parents of seven, expressed a sense of reassurance about the choices they had made. "Good, sound, constructive, consistent, loving discipline has actually built a bond between us and each of these children. You want them to be their best because you love them. We feel we have been on the right track with our disciplining, because all four of our married children are using basically the same methods."

Other parents said that their children basically accepted the discipline but that acceptance was often preceded by resistance or waiting, a "testing it out" or "thinking it over" period, and that usually the child ended up agreeing with the parents.

A small number of parents reported their children complied with the desired behavior after discipline but in such an angry and resentful mood that the experience it ended up being a generally negative one. "Pouting" was a problem with some of their eight children, confessed one Utah couple. The Idaho parents of four boys recall a consistent pattern of the children "arguing, debating, reasoning, and finally submitting" while the parents reciprocated by listening, reasoning with them, accepting their reasons as valid when they could, and negotiating more satisfactory solutions when they felt their children had a good point. About 20 percent said that they could not give one answer for all their children because some of them accepted discipline while others rejected it.

Even in these effective families, at least 5 percent of the parents reported that the general response to their discipline was rejection. Teenagers often seem to reject most methods of discipline. This fact is certainly one reason many parents feel teenagers are the hardest to rear.

Comparative Strictness

When parents were asked, "How strict are you in your family compared with other families you know?" the results were as follows:

Much stricter	17%
Somewhat stricter	54%
About the same	17%
Less strict	10%
Much less strict	2%

Since each family compared itself to other families they know, there is no way of knowing if there is any common standard of strictness. It is quite possible that in some regions "grounding" a child may be seen as very strict method, while in another community "grounding" is a standard practice and spanking a child or giving an angry scolding is considered strict.

It is also possible that strictness is seen as consistency of discipline. A strict family, by this definition, *always* applies discipline for an infraction. A less strict family overlooks infractions much of the time and only occasionally applies discipline. One parent put it this way: "I don't think we are a very strict family—at least when I compare our family with the way my dad handled us kids in my parents' home. But when I watch the way many of the children of our friends behave, I am astonished. We just would not allow our children to act that way. I see kids talking back to their parents, arguing, almost fighting, refusing point-blank to obey, staying out late without thinking of calling home, never seeming to do any work around the house—well, we just would not accept that kind of behavior. So, in comparison, I guess we are stricter. But we didn't have to talk about it to discipline the children because nobody did certain things. They especially didn't sass us. We had high expectations that everyone understood and met, but certainly we were not a rule-regulated family. We had a lot of freedom and flexibility, and as I look back on it, our children seldom abused the freedom we allowed."

A Provo, Utah, couple with three girls and four boys wrote: "From a strong base of commitment to each other and the gospel, a strong family is able to be very flexible about rules, patterns of life, and interactions with each other and the community. We feel that the love and nurturing the children get during their earliest years is critical in building that foundation. In our family, the mother was constantly available for preschool children because that was crucial, we felt, to their development. We also feel that having a sense of humor and not taking ourselves or each other too seriously have enabled us to enjoy each other, and to build a bond that enables us to be happy."

A California wife with four living daughters wrote with somewhat mingled humility and pride: "My husband's patriarchal blessing says that the children who would come into our family would be choice spirits, and they have been. I'm afraid the Lord would not trust us with any of his problem children. Our girls have just naturally seemed to want to do right. My husband's remarkable sense of humor has done much to make our home a happy place."

A Salt Lake City father with eight children observed,

"We're strict when it counts, yet we allow a lot of discretion. If we take a stand, we follow through to enforce it; however, we do not take stands lightly." Another couple explained, "Our family standards are higher than average but perceived discipline is less because family members generally do not need strictness."

"MUST-DO" REQUIREMENTS

We asked parents, "What are the things your children *must* do?" In addition to checking off the kinds of things they required from their children, many families wrote this kind of comment: "In our family there are very few things our children *must* do in the sense we absolutely require it. Particularly as our children get to the age of eight, we feel they have their free agency and should have the right to choose." Another wrote: "The word 'must' on your questionnaire is too strong for us. We do not make them do anything, but rely on the principle of free agency. Our children know that we use a pretty hefty amount of persuasion, though. We strongly encourage a lot of things but don't *make* them do anything in the final analysis." "We don't insist or force them to do any of these activities," wrote the Utah parents of nine, "but we encourage them to do all of them. They choose for themselves." A California couple with six children ran an eye over the list and admitted, "These are all 'musts' with room for exceptions and there have always been plenty of them."

Despite this pervasive sense of free agency, most

families felt that they had strong enough expectations that there was a sense of "must-do" for the following activities:

1. Go to church	76%
2. Help around the house	89%
3. Go to school every day	4%
4. Obey Church standards	82%
5. Live the Word of Wisdom	82%
6. Take part in family prayer	78%
7. Save for a mission	49%
8. Practice music lessons	51%

Among the other "must-do's" listed were working hard, saving money for their own needs and wants, speaking respectfully to parents, and respecting the rights of others.

It is interesting to note that school attendance is significantly ahead of the next-most emphasized activity, helping around the house. Going to school is a legal requirement as well as an expectation, and most parents feel they cannot let their children make a choice to stay home. Interestingly enough, one of the less-effective families wrote, "Our kids have to go to school every day unless we have something better to do. School isn't the only place to get an education, and we take them out a lot and do other things like skiing and fishing." While many effective families would agree that "school isn't the only place to get an education," probably very few of them would agree that recreation would be more important than school. All of these effective families expect their children to take rules seriously, and that includes family rules, Church principles, and the law.

MOTIVATIONS AND REWARDS

While discipline is sometimes seen as the negative, controlling side of child-rearing, positive attempts usually have the same end in mind: to increase desired behavior and reduce unwanted behavior. We also asked some questions about motivations so that we could make some appraisals of which methods seemed most effective.

We first asked parents, "Do you reward your children for some things?" Eighty-seven percent said yes; 13 percent said no. We then had them go over a list of rewards:

1. Praise		88%
2. Permission to do something special		72%
3. Money		43%
4. Trips		18%
5. TV time		10%
6. Other		11%

Parents jotted down such items as treats, special clothes, sports equipment, notes of appreciation, and even a reward of "trusting them with real responsibility."

The rewards seen as most effective, producing the best results, are praise (57 percent) and permission to do something special (15 percent). The Idaho parents of six explained that a real reward was "allowing [their children] more freedom to do things they wished to do [before they learned] responsibility. They have usually chosen good things." One Utah mother of seven cheerfully confessed, "I usually give money when I'm too tired to be creative and think of a reward that will build character."

"Love and approval is the reward they get, and they

appreciate it," said a significant number of parents.

"We did not set up an award system," said one couple. "We just gave what we had at the time. Sometimes it was a special meal or dessert. Other times it would be a rose, a treat, or a note left on a pillow or put on a plate."

"We would contract a reward for something accomplished," said other parents. "Our three sons achieved the Eagle rank. We agreed to pay half on a shotgun if they completed their Eagle. With another child, we agreed to get contact lenses if she finished reading the Doctrine and Covenants by age fourteen."

Several parents expressed concern about the "bribery" aspects of a rewards system, even though one couple frankly listed it among their "other" forms of discipline. One widowed Salt Lake City mother of five said, "I've always felt that rewards as such were not the best system. Children should do many things for the simple reward of accomplishment. We expect good grades and praise [the children)], but we don't bribe our children to get them. We might want to do things together after we've worked hard together on a project, but we don't hold up the reward of a movie or money as an incentive. When the children were little, perhaps we'd go out for ice cream or make cookies— something that particular child would especially enjoy, but we never decided on a reward ahead of time. We've tried to identify their feelings of joy when they've done something and praise *that*, make *that* the reward."

Another Salt Lake couple who adopted ten children use rewards in a combination of system and spontaneity. They keep party-favor surprises in a "treat bowl," and a youngster who manages to do something that he's been struggling with gets to pick one out. Other rewards are a night out alone with mom and dad, or a pizza party for the family. "Often," says this mother, "we give a reward just for love—because we just love the children and want to do something special for them."

Parents most frequently rewarded these actions:

1. Non-routine work (special achievements)	55%
2. Good grades	52%
3. Something that comes up we want our children to do	27%
4. Practicing music lessons	24%
5. Giving a talk	20%

Other rewarded behavior included no cavities, advancement in Scouting, a great effort in their activities and compassionate service.

A Texas couple with four children wrote: "Many of our children's friends have been rewarded for good grades with $1 or $5 for each "A." We have never felt this was a healthy approach. One of the best rewards we have found has been a family celebration. When one of the children brought home especially good grades, we took the whole family out to dinner to celebrate. It is good reinforcement when an older brother brags about how his younger brother's good grades are the source of a pleasant experience for the whole family, and we all look forward to the next grade period. Praise and rejoicing together over each others' accomplishments has been our best reward technique."

One Utah Valley couple takes their four sons out to dinner every quarter to celebrate good grades—but it's not a reward. They've never had low grades. In one Utah family with seven children, giving talks, getting good grades, and going to church are expected "therefore no material rewards are given." Other parents would probably agree. "We tend to give rewards spontaneously, after the fact," said one couple. "We don't routinely hand out rewards in an attempt to foster improved behavior." Even here, however, flexibility paid off. With one child, money was the most successful motivation for achieving a goal.

Often the parents would plan how the reward system was going to work and make it correspond with the goals they set, within the framework of their family values. "We really use the rewards in diverse ways for each family member," wrote one couple. "As we talk together, we discuss each child and try to come up with something that will help him or her move in the proper direction. For one it may be a reward to get her to work on her music, as we think she has a pretty good talent with that. For others it is a reward to help them pick up their grades a little bit. Sometimes the children complain when another child gets a reward that they would like, but we tend to ignore that. The children have been told that we try to personalize the rewards to help them do better, and they know that in the end they all about even out."

These effective Mormon families have high expectations, a few rules, and an occasional struggle, whether they use positive or negative means to obtain compliance. We asked two of our final questions to see how well parents thought they had done. They were to check the appropriate blank: (1) "In general, we think our family is very special, about average for the families we know, or not as good as most families we know." (2) "How does your family compare with your own ideals and expectations for your family?"

Eighty-nine percent of the parents checked the "very

special" place on the first question; 10 percent checked "about average for the families we know"; and only 1 percent checked "not as good as most families we know."

In answer to the second question, 75 percent of these parents said that their families met their expectations. Twenty-three percent said that their family fell "somewhat short of our expectations." But only 1 percent responded that it fell "very short" of their expectations. (One percent did not respond.) One of the couples who said their family fell somewhat short is a family with seven children, two of which are divorced and two of which failed to graduate from high school. This couple commented: "I think as a family we've learned that the principle of free agency is very important; and when you reject it, you're taking a course that will afterwards bring some sorrow. However, as a family we've learned about unconditional love and caring and never giving up. We're not the typical wonderful family that boasts of every child a missionary and all married in the temple, but we've had enough adversity to help us be compassionate to others in difficulties (there are a lot of them in the Church) and enough of seeing children change to give us hope. We've learned that life is always going to be a test. There's never a time when you are through with the hard things and can relax."

TEACHING BY PRECEPT AND EXAMPLE

Several of the parents in our study cited a well-known quotation of Joseph Smith about his method of governing the Saints. "I teach them correct principles and they govern themselves." The Lord has assigned parents the responsibility to teach their children, and these parents accept it. Another favorite quotation is: "Inasmuch as parents have children in Zion, or in any of her stakes which are organized, that teach them not to understand the doctrine of repentance, faith in Christ the Son of the living God, and of baptism and the gift of the Holy Ghost by the laying on of the hands, when eight years old, the sin be upon the heads of the parents (D&C 68:25.)."

LDS children, to some extent, live in two worlds: the gospel-centered world of the Church and the achievement-oriented world of secular society. Sometimes these two worlds are seen as compatible, sometimes not. The family and Church classes are the primary areas of instruction in the first world. Public education is the primary means of instruction in the second. The effective parents in this study consider themselves responsible in both spheres to help their children succeed.

We asked a cluster of questions designed to show what parents do in both areas:

1. How do you teach your children? (We suggested: talk to them regularly, try to set a good example, hold regular family home evenings, read scriptures together regularly, and "other.")
2. About how many hours per week do each of you watch television?(Include only the children at home).
3. How many hours each week do you watch television together?
4. Do you control what programs the children can watch?
5. Which Church magazines do you subscribe to?
6. How many of you in the family usually read at least half of the *Ensign, New Era,* and *Friend*?
7. What kinds of books do you have in your home? (We suggested "a lot" of Church books, "a few" Church books, literary books, dictionaries, encyclopedia, history books, atlases, biographies, and "other.")

TEACHING ACTIVITIES

We asked parents, "How do you teach your children?" Following are the responses:

1. Try to set a good example	100%
2. Talk to them regularly	94%
3. Try to hold family night regularly	63%

4. Read scriptures together regularly   34%
5. Other: look for teaching moments,
   encourage reading Church books   20%

Many parents added explanations about the top two methods, clearly the favored ones, and, they felt, their most effective teaching methods. "When we go out to build fences or work with the machinery, we talk together as father and sons," said one ranching father. "Sometimes we talk about the gospel and my mission. Sometimes we talk about political issues and things that are happening in the world. And sometimes we just work."

Ninety-nine percent of the parents said they always pay their tithing; 97 percent always attend Church meetings; and 93 percent always accept Church callings and assignments. Furthermore, 97 percent of them said they actively try to help neighbors in need. The result is that their children see a model of rendering service to others. Over 98.8 percent of these couples were married in the temple or were sealed after a civil wedding. Both father and mother have a personal commitment to education (80 percent of the fathers and 70 percent of the mothers had attended college). They are very active in fulfilling Church callings, and they emphasize the importance of the family by the amount of time they spend with their children. Clearly, as far as Church commitment is concerned, the parents expect to be their children's primary models.

Sixty-six percent of the families said they hold a weekly family home evening "usually" or "always," but only 28 percent say they "usually" or "always" read the scriptures regularly. From this, we infer that the parents do most of their teaching in informal settings. Actually, this is quite logical. Family home evening is only once a week, but informal talks or discussions seem to occur almost every day. When we asked parents what they did regularly together in the family, this is how they responded:

1. Talk together	always 64%	usually 31%
2. Do (play) things together	always 61%	usually 35%
3. Do household chores together	always 32%	usually 40%
4. Discuss family problems together	always 52%	usually 40%

These families see themselves as spending a considerable amount of time together talking, discussing problems, and doing things together. Doing household chores together is lower than we might have guessed, but at least one family from Idaho listed "working together" as one of their most effective teaching techniques, while a Utah Valley couple with five children "always worked with the children on household or yard chores to teach them properly." One Utah couple with seven children ranging in age from eighteen to thirty-three recalled, "We not only have always played and prayed together, but we have had some of our best teaching moments *working* as a family."

Several parents included examples of the kinds of values they taught. "Sometimes in our prayers we will address a specific problem and ask for divine guidance in helping to understand or cope with a situation," one couple observed. Working out the problem, then, constitutes a built-in basis for discussion. "We have used important events in the extended family as times for discussions; for example, mission farewells and homecomings, temple marriages, blessings, baptisms, Scouting advancements, and family reunions," say another couple.

An Idaho couple with ten closely spaced children remains alert to "take advantage of the teaching moments that come daily." "Whenever questions arise, we go to our reference books and find an answer." They also have lively mealtime conversations dealing with current events and recent lessons from Church and school classes.

Similarly, another couple has the practice of talking "with our children about the lessons they have been given in Seminary, Primary, Sunday School, and so on. A common table topic at dinner is 'what did you talk about in your class today?'"

"Often we will take a certain person (church leader, current-event figure) and talk about that person and look at what we can learn (either positive or negative) from their example," said the parents of another family. "Sometimes we will just talk about the good things in the lives of those who live around us."

A Texas couple and their four children have a tradition of "piling on the parents' bed and talking—making plans, sharing ideas, setting goals, swapping experiences." "That's probably our best teaching technique." A Montana biologist and his wife found that the family council with their four children was an effective place to teach. A Utah couple worked consciously to ensure that their eight children "have growing experiences inside and outside the house."

One Wyoming couple with six children gave them responsibility "at an early age and then held them accountable." They commented that this was one of their most effective teaching methods.

SCHOOL

We asked parents in our sample about their own schooling. Husbands averaged 16.0 years—coming out to exactly four years of college and wives averaged 13.8, or almost two years of college. When we asked them to appraise their children's scholastic performance, about 66 percent reported that their children had above-average grades.

One couple said, "We try to talk with our children's teachers to see how they are doing and what we can do in the home to support what the teacher is trying to get across." They did this with the children's Primary, priesthood, and MIA classes as well. One Salt Lake City family with five children, the father of whom is a technician and the mother a secretary, have made academics a high priority. They have "one Sterling Scholar, one nominee, and one working for it" among their children.

One mother of four, who said her children were "very easy to teach" and had "never given us worry or heartaches," observed: "Our children have not been leaders in student government or high achievers such as Sterling Scholars, though they have all averaged high grades in school and received several scholarships."

READING AND TELEVISION

We asked our parents to identify their reading and

television habits for two reasons: We wanted to research some of the attitudes they had toward education (reading is usually a fundamental) and to see how they handled the potentially controversial issue of television.

More than two-thirds of the highly effective parents felt that their home libraries were above average in the neighborhood. The breakdown is as follows:

1. Much better than most neighbors	34%
2. Better than most neighbors	35%
3. About the same as most neighbors	26%

One Utah mother of five, who checked "better than most" observed in the margin. "We're always loaning books."

What kinds of books do these families have in their home libraries? Almost every home has a dictionary and an encyclopedia, and about 80 percent have an atlas. In these homes, Church books occupy an important place—99 percent said the home library included "a lot" of such volumes. Literature—novels, poetry, adventure, Westerns, science fiction, and essays—appeared in about 80 percent of the libraries, followed by history and biography in two-thirds of the home libraries. Parents also mentioned cookbooks, game and joke books, "how-to" books, foreign language books, children's books, and books dealing with science, Scouting, politics, business, art, music, and special fields. Some families also mentioned "heavy" traffic in and out of the public library, or made a comment like, "We read a lot." One Utah couple with a professor father and college-graduate mother checked everything and then jotted down, "We have tons of books of all kinds."

Church magazines formed a good share of the reading. Ninety-two percent of the families took the *Ensign*, and 46 percent read at least half of the magazine. (Only 2 percent "never read" at least half.) Eighty-four percent of the families took the *New Era*, and 52 percent read at least half. (Only 3 percent "never read" at least half.) Forty-three percent of the families took the *Friend*—probably reflecting the age distribution of the children. Forty-one percent read at least half. (Only 5 percent "never read" half.) Several couples also listed such Mormon-oriented publications as *This People* and *Church News*. Besides Church magazines, the average family also subscribed to four other publications. Most frequently mentioned were *National Geographic*, *Time* or *Newsweek*, *Reader's Digest*, and *Better Homes and Gardens*. Many homes would also include a specialty publication connected with the father's work (*Chemical Engineer*, *Money*), a special interest of the parents (*Farm Journal Workbasket*, *Golf Digest*, *NEA Journal*), and other magazines geared to the interests of the children, such as *Popular Mechanics*, *Boy's Life*, *Sports Illustrated*, *Byte*, *Compute!* or *Seventeen*.

One Montana family with a contractor father, homemaker mother, and only two of six children still at home (boys seven and fifteen) subscribed to all three Church magazines as well as *Reader's Digest*, *Smithsonian*, *National Geographic*, *U.S. News & World Report*, *Hot Rod*, *Oceans*, *Montana Outdoor*, *Church News*, *World*, *Ladies Home Journal*, *McCall's*, *Better Homes and Gardens*, *Freeman*, and *Prevention*. A Utah family with seven children subscribes to more than twenty magazines, including two on pigeon racing and five on horse racing. Additionally, almost all the families interviewed reported that they subscribed to a daily newspaper. Our study did not ask who in the family read what or how much, but the evidence is clear that parents in these homes have a generous supply of good reading available for the family members.

When it comes to television watching, our sample showed a strikingly low number of hours compared to a national sample. Our study showed that on an average day, the parents and children at home watched television for an hour and four minutes. A national survey in 1982 showed almost triple that time: two hours and fifty-one minutes a day median time. (Robert T. Bower, *The Changing Television Audience in America* [New York: Columbia University College, 1985].) When we looked only at the college-educated portion of our sample, they watched only 55 minutes compared to the 1982 national sample of two hours and eighteen minutes. We tried to break the pattern down even further; here's what the data show:

Children between two and five watched twenty-seven hours and nine minutes a week in a sample collected by the Nielsen rating. Our sample watched eight hours and thirty-six minutes. Children between six and eleven from the national sample watched twenty-four hours and fifty minutes, while ours watched eleven hours and forty-two minutes. Starting at age twelve, we broke the figures down to see if there were any differences between male and female viewing patterns. Teenage boys in the national sample watched twenty-five hours and seventeen minutes, while ours watched nine hours and twenty-four minutes. For girls, the time was almost identical. The national sample watched television for twenty-four hours and sixteen minutes while the teenage girls in our sample watched for nine hours and twenty-nine minutes.

Young adults between eighteen and thirty-four showed an even greater divergence from the national sample. Young men in the national sample watched twenty-eight hours and thirty minutes, compared to five hours and fifty-seven minutes in our sample while young women in the national sample watched thirty hours and nineteen minutes compared with our sample of six hours and twenty-two minutes. During the highly productive years of thirty-five to fifty-four, when most adults are juggling the responsibilities of work and rearing their families, the national sample of men watched an average of twenty-seven hours and fifty minutes compared to our sample of ten hours and eighteen minutes. The national sample of women watched thirty-three hours and twenty-three minutes. The women in our sample actually watched less than the men, with seven hours and twenty-four minutes. The biggest gap, however, occurs in the retirement years. American men over fifty-five watch television an average of thirty-five hours and fifty-three minutes, while our sample was seeing six hours and six minutes; women of the same age were up to forty-one hours and thirteen minutes—the equivalent of a full working week—while women in our sample tuned in their sets an average of six hours and twenty-four minutes. (*Trends in Attitudes Toward Television and Other Media: A Twenty-four Year Report by the Roper Organization.* 5B:84, April 1983; *Public Perceptions of Television and Other Mass Media: A Twenty-Year Review, 1959 1967: A Report by the Roper Organization,* April 1979.)

In our sample of highly effective families, most of the television viewing was done by the children between six and eleven by an impressively large margin, while young adults watched the least amount of television. At most, however, members of highly effective families are watching less than half the national average number of hours and, at the point of widest divergence, only one-eighth as much. About 5 percent of the parents we surveyed said they did not watch television at all during the week. One Utah family with six children from ten to twenty-five logged barely an hour's viewing time a day for everyone except for the seventeen-year-old, who had medical problems and whose viewing was about ten hours a week.

In general, watching television together is not an important activity that the family does together. Fifty-four percent of the families said they watched television together as a family two hours or less a week. One Washington family with six children explained, "We do not watch television often because we find other activities, especially reading, more interesting." Another 37 percent said they watched less than ten hours a week as a family. The Provo parents of nine wrote: "When our twins were asked what their favorite television show was, on a school survey, they wrote 'The News.' They were eight years old. This was probably because we all watch the news together and discuss the day's events."

One mother observed, "Sometimes we watch television as a family, and sometimes I listen to it a little as background noise when I am home alone doing the ironing or other work. I seldom ever really look at it, however. About the only thing that we consistently watch is the news and the Choir broadcast on some Sundays." Several women mentioned having the television on as "background" while they did housework.

When we asked parents if they controlled what their children watched, they answered:

1. Always	24%
2. Often	38%
3. Sometimes	21%
4. Seldom	10%
5. Never	7%

However, the matter of control means different things to different people. One Provo family of five commented that the television had always gone off after supper until homework was finished, unless an exceptional program was on. One father said: "We don't check up on what programs our kids watch. However, we have talked about television programming, and our children know the kinds of programs we don't approve of. Since we can't check every program they watch (and don't want to), we feel we must tell our children our standards of television programming and trust them to control their own television watching."

A Wyoming couple commented, "Our family seems to choose good programs. If we comment that a show is unfit or if the children see material that they know is not appropriate, they don't watch it."

A Wyoming forest ranger and his wife do not monitor what their children watch, but they decided against cable television, and they screen the videos the children are allowed to watch. A Provo couple with seven children seldom control programming: "We suggest; they choose," is the way they put it.

Although our study did not probe this area in depth, the comments of the parents indicated that they had thought through how they wanted their children to relate to television and felt comfortable with their decisions. In contrast, one of the less-effective families indicated dissatisfaction and vagueness: "Our kids watch way too much television. I guess we shouldn't let them do it like they do."

CULTURAL EXPOSURE

One couple wrote, "We have read to our children extensively from birth, and we talk about what we have read. We have used books and observation to learn about trees, flowers, birds, animals, and a whole range of subjects."

Another couple corroborated, "It is important to us that our children learn something about the elements of good culture. We have tried to have good music and paintings in the home. We keep books and have a recommended reading list. Then we take our children to concerts, plays, seminars". Another couple said, "When we travel or even on short trips, we try to visit places of interest. We have gone to historical places of interest to the Church or the country. We may visit a museum, an art gallery, a beautiful building or natural setting." A couple of families have reading lists of suggested books, or find books on interesting topics that come up. In a Utah family with seven children, the mother, a piano teacher, wrote: "We started at an early age to steer our kids toward appreciating better music and away from rock. We feel terrific about how they respond to classical music."

In one Provo family of seven where the father is a

professor and composer and the mother is a homemaker and student, the family works together on reports and projects. The children "have had many hours of reading from their mother," and they take walks together. "We sustain excitement about learning and accomplishments," they wrote. In another family of seven, also from Provo, the parents deliberately include good music and great paintings as part of the home environment.

Music lessons, as a reflection of family culture, received a high share of comments. Several parents commented that they had tried rewarding their children for practicing, often unsuccessfully. Another couple required that the children pay the teacher, but then paid the children for practicing, a rather ingenious rule. Another family had a rule that "every child must learn something about music. He or she can choose the instrument to play, but must be involved in music lessons and practice for two years. After that they can choose to continue or stop."

An Idaho farm couple with four sons and three daughters observed that practicing music lessons was expected and required but "needed rewards" to really work.

Although family educational goals in our survey differed from family to family, a general pattern is clear. Highly effective parents feel comfortable in their role as their children's teachers, whether that role involves giving them the skills, structure, and discipline they need to succeed in school; explaining and implementing gospel principles; consciously exposing them to important cultural elements; or reinforcing the children's own learning efforts. They consider themselves responsible for helping their children become well educated. They also consider themselves to be the primary conveyors of religious values.

SHOWING CONSTANT AFFECTION

Because love has always been part of the pattern of happy family life, and because the parents in this survey ranked love with gospel commitment as one of two important elements in their successful family life, we wanted to know more about what that meant.

Do loving families express love verbally? By hugs? By kisses? By doing kind things for each other? Do they always treat each other with respect? At one point Christ said to his disciples, "If ye love me, keep my commandments (John 14:15)." Should we expect to find more obedience in families where members say they love each other? In Doctrine and Covenants 121:41-43 says that power and influence should only be exercised by "love unfeigned," and that if reproof is given, it should be followed by an "increase of love." How do highly effective couples teach family love to their children?

We asked the following questions:

1. How do you express love in your family? (Responses we offered are listed with percentages below.)

2. Please rank these ways of expressing love.

While the data gathered may not give us complete answers to all of our questions, it is possible to identify certain trends:

1. Tell them we love them	97%
2. Do things for them	96%
3. Hugging	94%
4. Tell by writing or phoning	91%
5. Kissing	85%
6. Provide a living for them	74%

Answers in the "other" category seemed into cluster in a couple of major areas:

Getting together, talking, sharing, supporting	72%
Teasing and joking	20%

We also asked parents to rank in order their various expressions of love, and then to indicate which they did first, second, third, and so on. Below is listed each expression and what percentage of the respondents ranked it first and second.

1. Telling	62% first	24% second
2. Doing things for	40% first	33% second
3. Hugging	17% first	24% second
4. Kissing	12% first	7% second
5. Write or phone	12% first	7% second
6. Provide for	8% first	12% second

These families indicated that telling that you love someone—either face-to-face, by phone, or in writing–is most important. Next in importance is doing things for a loved one, followed by touching them.

As this tabulation shows, 94 percent of the families indicated that hugging was a part of family expressions of love, and 85 percent said that kissing was. Hugging was the most popular form of physical affection mentioned, with kissing occurring 10 percent less often. Still, it seems that there are some good families that have little or no physical expressions of love and affection. Although both hugs and kisses were among the top seven, they were not the top two. About 17 percent said that kissing would be the last method for showing love, and 7 percent said that hugging would be last.

It is not possible to tell what constitutes a hug or a kiss in these families. When we asked people to be more descriptive during interviews, we got definitions of a hug ranging from a two-armed, full-body embrace to putting an arm around the shoulders. Kissing might be a generous smack on the lips or a peck on the cheek. Bishop H. Burke Peterson, formerly of the First Council of Seventy, and his brothers have a habit of kissing each other on the lips whenever they meet. This pattern would be absolutely foreign to many other equally good families. President Spencer W. Kimball was almost legendary for his overflowing love, which manifested itself (outside his family as well as inside) with a kiss on the cheek, an affectionate hug, or holding the hand of someone he was talking to.

It would be interesting to check perceptions with the children in our sample to see if they felt love being communicated as the parents meant to communicate it. One mother, who indicated that "doing things" for her children was a primary mode of showing affection, commented, "I don't think my children will ever appreciate how much we love them and how much we sacrificed and did for them until they have children of their own. When they are up all night with a sick child, frantic with fear, or when they go to work the next day heavy with fatigue, or when they spend the few dollars on toys for the kids rather than something for the parents—maybe then they will remember that we did all of the same things for them." Perhaps she is right, and perceptions of behavior as love develop more over time.

None of the survey responses suggested that affection was not important. One Utah couple with four children checked everything and wrote in the margin, "This is what it's all about!" An Idaho farming couple with seven children wrote, "These are all important. Our family has needed them all depending on age and circumstances." The Provo mother of nine children explained that "the boys wrestle with their father in a fun way." But she added, "All the forms of affection are interrelated. You can't have one without the other. We do feel it is very important to express our love for each other often."

One Utah father of five, four of whom are sons, deliberately patterned physical affection into the family structure. He wrote: "I think we're an affectionate family—at least, we hug and kiss a lot as family members come and go and at special events. When our children were young, we gave them lots of physical affection; but as the boys got older, they seemed somewhat embarrassed if we kissed them, especially in front of their friends. I tended to back off a little, although their mother still kissed them. It was nice to have a daughter, because she liked to be hugged and kissed and I enjoyed doing it. But I didn't like never touching my boys either, and I found they liked it when I'd sneak up behind them and grab them in a big bear hug or start a mock tussle. Later, I decided to kiss them as I left on a trip and returned, or if they were going somewhere. I talked with them about it, and aside from the initial awkwardness of starting the custom, it has become an accepted family practice. We still do it, and all of the children are married now."

Many parents wrote comments that showed their family had created a "family definition" of love. One Utah family added that they showed love by "forgiving." Another Utah couple wrote: "Love is service to one another, feeling or showing that you care through actions, showing interest in, and involvement in, each of their individual activities, interests, projects, and friends." An Idaho family with ten children also had little family traditions of "winking across the room, holding hands, or blowing a kiss." Another Idaho family added "honoring birthdays, family jokes, and stories" to the list of how they showed affection, while "being together" and "talking to (the children) with respect and appreciation" were high on other families' lists. A Utah couple with seven children also added "pats, backrubs, teasing, horseplay, and special family home evenings to honor someone." A Texas couple with four children simply said, "Surprises!"

Traditionally, parenting has meant providing. We included a question about providing a living to see how strong this belief still was. Some parents were puzzled by the question and jotted down an explanatory note that the children were "on their own now" or that "this went without saying." One of the less-effective fathers, interestingly enough, responded to it directly by saying, "We don't show any affection in our family. Oh, I think that we love each other most of the time, but we just don't show it. I guess just making a living for the children ought to be an expression of love for them. Lots of families don't even provide for themselves." A Provo couple indicated that they showed love by "providing educational opportunities" for their children and "going places together."

One mother said, "I do many things out of love for my children. I will fix a meal early or make a lunch when they have to go to work. I will iron a dress or shirt, provide refreshments for a party, pick up after them if they are busy. I feel I do many things for my children because I love them. But I am not always sure they recognize what I have done or if they really appreciate it.

When we did follow-up interviews with some families, we found differences in the ease and openness families felt in expressing love. Several of the questionnaires indicated some inhibition about physical affection. In one California family, the parents hugged and kissed, but one child did not like to be kissed.

More frequently, it was the mother and father who had different feelings about hugs and kisses. One mother said, "The father by nature is not a hugger or a kisser." In one family, the parents indicated that neither hugs nor kisses were part of their repertoire and explained, "We're just not the type." Both parents grew up in homes where physical affection was not common. They found other ways to communicate affection for their children. In a follow-up interview, they agreed that there was a lot of love in the home but that "it gets expressed in other ways."

Some couples indicated that a common way of expressing love was with the "me too" response. If one member of the family told another that she loved them, the other's response would be "me too." In some families, it seems difficult to freely say, "I really love and appreciate you."

The interviews also revealed that in some families the most open expressions of love and appreciation came through the public forum of ward testimony meetings. Often a husband or wife could more easily express deep feelings of love and appreciation in a meeting than in a private, face-to-face encounter. One reason may be that there would be no possibility of rejection or interruption during the meeting; and while a child might feel squirmy or embarrassed, he or she would not feel required to respond in some way when the parent finishes. The public setting, in a way, becomes a method of safeguarding privacy.

Children also used this public forum to express feelings of tenderness and appreciation that they might otherwise keep to themselves. More than one couple said, "The first time I heard our son say he loved us was at his missionary farewell."

We also asked parents how often members of their family showed physical affection to one another. The results were:

1. Daily		81%
2. Weekly		9%
3. Monthly		2%
4. Never		1%

Since this question did not ask couples to specify which form of affection was used on these occasions, it could range from a hug or a kiss to a pat on the back, a touch, a routine greeting or goodnight kiss. It could also include a warmly affectionate conversation with horseplay ,or lots of hugs.

In a family's life span, the pattern of showing affection seems to change and develop. Our general impression is that in American culture, kissing and hugging is commonplace in most families when children are young, but decreases as children get older. It also seems more culturally acceptable for daughters to continue to kiss both parents than for boys. A son, now forty, who was interviewed during the follow-up phase, recalled the pattern in his family of thirteen children: "When I was small my parents would always kiss me, but as I grew older my mother would kiss me, but father did only on special occasions, like when I went into military service. Then as I got older, I had left home, of course, and I would always kiss both of my parents when I saw them. My sisters did all along, but I don't think that any of the other brothers did."

Most families indicated that they "of course" hugged and kissed an adult child on landmark occasions—when he or she left for college or on a long trip, at a wedding, at graduation, or at a time of special recognition. They also responded this way when a child was ill or emotionally upset, no matter what his or her age.

It seems remarkable that so basic an area of family interaction has never been studied with a national sample, but there is simply no data available for comparison. A recent study of BYU students shows very little physical affection expressed between fathers and sons, except when the sons are very small. There is significantly more affection between fathers and daughters. It seems logical to expect some generational differences to develop, with families of the future being more openly affectionate. The new emphasis in the nation as well as in the Church on involving fathers more actively in the actual work of caring for infants and toddlers may make them feel more comfortable about continuing to hug and kiss them as they grow.

Certainly, the absence of ways to express physical affection appropriately must be related in some way to the shocking rates of father-daughter incest in this country and the widely publicized correlation (though not necessarily a causal relationship) between homosexual men and emotionally aloof fathers. Some serious family specialists have encouraged more appropriate physical affection between dads and boys, dads and daughters, and other members of the family. There is no way to measure the tragedy of normal, healthy affection between parents and offspring that must manifest itself in joyless, abnormal, and even violent ways.

TEACHING THE VALUE OF WORK AND MONEY

Another characteristic of strong Mormon families is that children are expected to work and strive to learn a strong work ethic. It did not surprise us that the work ethic was more evident as children worked for wages outside the home than when they did chores at home. Our own children exhibited the same pattern.

We first wanted to know what kinds of activities these families engaged in, and where work fit into the family activity pattern.

FAMILY ACTIVITIES

We asked families to identify activities that they consider to be very important in their families and that family members usually have a strong interest in doing. Following are the top items for activities strongly emphasized *within* the family:

1. Travel	77%
2. Playing musical instruments	75%
3. Sports (outside of school)	74%
4. Parties in the home	67%
5. Sewing	60%
6. Singing in the home	50%
7. Hobbies	41%
8. Fishing and hunting	40%

We also asked parents to identify what their children did *outside* the family. They responded as follows:

1. Boy or Girl Scouts	85%
2. Earning money outside the home	83%
3. Sports in school	75%
4. Academic interests	74%
5. Playing musical instruments	71%
6. Going to dances	71%
7. Having dates	70%
8. Speaking in public or debating	56%
9. Holding office in school	53%
10. Singing in public	51%
11. Parties outside the home	48%
12. Being in plays or drama	44%

It was interesting that the second-most-important reason children were not home was that they were employed. Usually, these children were not driven to work by poverty. When we asked these families to rate their incomes as above, about the same, or below that of their neighbors, 60 percent of them reported higher-level incomes. A more important reason for working children is that their highly effective parents have a strong work ethic.

They teach their children good work habits, encourage them to work, and want them to experience the satisfaction of earning their own money. One mother reported, "All of our children have been expected to work around the house even when they were small. As they got older, we didn't actually force them to get a summer job or to work on Saturdays or after school, but all of the children knew that they would have a lot more money to spend if they earned it than if they always came to us for a handout."

How did these parents teach work values? And how did they handle the problems involved in getting children to do their share of the household chores? We asked these questions:

1. Have your children obtained jobs outside the family while they were still living at home?
2. If you require your children to work around the home, how much time, on the average, do you require each week for the following ages? ____5-10 years____11-15 years ____16-20 years ____21-25 years.
3. Which kinds of jobs do your girls do? (We offered a list that included yard work, dishes, cleaning, work in the garden or on the farm, work with animals, helping can, cooking, fixing the house, fixing the automobile,and "other.")
4. Do you have family projects? (We listed gardening, genealogy, memorizing poetry or scriptures, working on the house, working in the family business, doing missionary work, doing service projects, and "other.")
5. Do you give your children an allowance?
6. Do you require your children to work for money they get from you?

7. About how many dollars per week do you give your children at the following ages? 6-10 years? $___11-15 years? $___16-20 years? $___21 and over but not married? $___

8. Do you help your married children in any of these ways? Giving money as gifts, giving money as loans, providing child care while they work, doing occasional babysitting, offering advice, giving blessings, and "other."

In answering the question about requiring household chores, 77 percent of the parents responded that children did at least some of the household chores on the list. A surprisingly high 60 percent said that children did these chores willingly. "Most of the time," added one conscientious father of five. A Utah father of seven penned in, "Sometimes. Kids are kids." A Utah couple with five children added, "We never expect them to do something we would not do ourselves," and a Utah couple with eight children acknowledged, "Our children are above average in their attitude, but they did not always do household chores without occasional feelings of unfairness."

We had asked an question earlier about "the things that your children *must* do." Many of the parents rephrased the question in terms of expectations rather than requirements, and almost 90 percent said that helping with the family chores is an expectation in the family rather than a reality.

One mother explained the problem this way: "We have tried to get our kids to help around the house, and we have tried everything—restricting TV, paying for work done, grounding, scolding—but nothing has worked for very long. The kids get busy, and I find it really easier to do it myself than to get into a hassle with the children.

One Provo father of six recalls the chore and allowance dilemma as a consistent frustration: "This was always a bugaboo for us. We tried every scheme imaginable to get our children to work in the home, and nothing was too successful. TV was used as a reward, and that worked for a time. We tried putting out a list of jobs in the home with the amount to be earned for each task. That just didn't work. The children said they didn't need money when we needed work done. We finally came to the point that we provided money as it was needed and tried to get agreements with each child as to that child's fair share of the family work. It's some comfort now to discover that many other good families struggle through the same issue. My wife has also found out that she isn't the only mother who moved in and silently did a child's chores when she felt that the child was struggling with a heavy schedule or a problem with a friend. But we were probably too lenient in requiring work around the house. If a child was busy in some other legitimate activity, we nearly always excused him or her from the chores."

We asked parents how much time they expected children to work each week around the home. The results are listed below by the ages of children, the average time expected, and the most frequently listed time. This third listing is important. For example, for ages five to ten, most families expect only two hours of work a week. However, some families, usually farm families, expect much more, so the average is much higher—four hours a week.

Age Listed by Respondents	Average Hours of Work Expected Per Week	Expected by Most Families
5-10 years	4 hours	2 hours
11-15 years	7 hours	4 hours
16-20 years	9 hours	4 and 10 hours
21-28 years	11 hours	2 hours

The group of children between sixteen and twenty actually has two frequently listed hours of work completion–four and ten hours. Again, the difference is clearly related to where the family lives. Urban children who have a heavy schedule of academics, sports, other lessons, recreation, and easily accessible friends are expected to work at home only four hours a week. Rural families with the demands of crops and animals require more hours of work from their children and usually answered ten hours. One farm mother explained, "Our children have always been willing to assist with the home and farm work. Most of the families in the community seem to have about the same pattern. Everyone works. Some, of course, seem to let their children get by with doing less, but our whole community works and seems to believe in it. As we have watched the children get older and leave home, we see the most success from those who had responsibility and had to work. Work is just part of life."

The reports on children ages twenty-one to twenty-five still living at home are too varied to produce a common pattern. Only forty-five families out of the 200 still had children of that age living at home. Usually, missions, work, school, or marriage have taken them away. In some of the families, children in this age group had almost complete responsibility for taking care of the home. Others working full time had almost no chores. Thus, our data is misleading when it shows that the average amount of time expected for this older group is eleven hours a week, and the time most frequently checked is two hours. One mother whose twenty-three-year-old son was living at home and working full time said: "Now that he is working full time, we expect very little from him in helping around the house. In fact, we would be delighted if he would just make his bed and keep his own room picked up. He is a great young man (returned missionary) and we want him to save his money and get married, so we do not charge him room and board. I don't think he realizes how much additional work he creates. He thinks since he is gone to work all day and out most evenings that he doesn't have much impact in the home. But I still do his laundry, fix his meals, make his lunch, and pick up after him and his friends when they are here. There is a lot more work than he thinks."

A substantial number of parents jotted down explanatory comments about how much or how little their children worked, at what, and how willingly.

"In our family there was no set number of hours children were expected to work each week. Everyone was expected to pitch in, an we all keep the house neat and clean. The house is cleaned for the day before everyone leaves for school or work. We have breakfast together, family prayer, and sometimes scripture reading."

"The amount of time children work at home is difficult to measure," observed one Provo couple with nine children ranging from ages nine to twenty-two. "In the summertime, those at home work one to four hours per day. As they get older, they get jobs away from home and they spend less time working at home.

One Utah couple doesn't give their fourteen children allowances or pay them for working. They said, "We want our children to learn how to work in the family without feeling, 'What will you give me for it?' or 'How much is it worth?' "They also required a substantial amount of work per week from their children: seven hours for children under ten, ten hours for children under fifteen, and twelve hours for children between sixteen and twenty.

"In our family each person is responsible for some personal things—room and clothes," wrote another couple. "Then we usually all work together until what we need to do is finished."

One couple controlled the amount of time spent in work because they wanted the children to do other things: "We had a bulletin board with the jobs each person was assigned to do after school. We varied jobs from time to time so one person didn't always do the same thing. But once the children finished their work, we did not add to the list. They need time for some play and homework. "In another family, academic interests and doing well in school were extremely important to the parents. "To provide study time for six children, we gave them a break at home—so Mother did more of the work than in many families," they wrote.

A Salt Lake City family with seven living children took a middle position. "All of our children have delivered the paper from age eight. This has always provided them with their spending money until they choose to earn more," wrote their mother. "But we think that their senior year is soon enough to work at more than odd jobs. Too much money too soon makes them too independent when they are not always wise. There's a time for everything; and we want them to enjoy and learn during high school—not earn." This same family also puts a limit on housework: They clean one floor of their two-story house on Thursday and the other floor on Friday. Then they use Saturday as a "fun day."

Interestingly, a mother in one of the less-effective families commented, "Our kids are all involved in the farm, but the kids hate it because their dad is a workaholic." Incidentally, the term, "workaholic" did not appear in any of the discussions about work among the highly effective families.

"MEN'S WORK" AND "WOMEN'S WORK"

We wondered how traditional these highly effective families were, and if strict gender roles were part of the family pattern. For that reason, we asked parents which chores boys did and which chores girls did. Interestingly enough, most of these homes showed a very egalitarian approach to work:

Jobs	Girls Only	Boys Only	Both
1. Yard work 4%	23%	71%	
2. Doing dishes	23%	2%	76%
3. House cleaning	21%	1%	77%
4. Work in garden or farm	4%	18%	78%
5. Work with animals	4%	21%	75%
6. Cooking	42%	2%	55%
7. Fixing the house	8%	40%	52%

8. Fixing the car	1%	86%	13%

Out of all of these activities, only "fixing the car" is clearly seen as men's work. For all of the rest, over half of the responses indicate that the activity is considered appropriate for both boys and girls. One Idaho couple with three children wrote down "sewing and mending" as another activity and said that it was required of their two boys as well as their daughter. Other families specified that child care was required of both boys and girls, while a Provo family of seven also involved both sons and daughters in grocery shopping, typing, doing the laundry, and balancing the checkbook."

The responses did indicate preferences for girls doing dishes, house cleaning, and cooking, while boys more often did yard work, farm or garden work, animal care, or fix-it projects. But it is possible to see in this pattern that getting the work done–not worrying who does it—is the important value.

Some of the comments parents added to this part of the survey indicated an unconscious awareness of gender in the family's work patterns. "As long as our children lived at home, they made their own beds and kept their rooms straight," wrote one couple. "The boys took out the garbage and did the yards. The girls helped with meals and general housework. Sometimes they would have to fit these chores into their schedules, so jobs were not always done at the same time."

One Texas family with four daughters and three sons checked everything in duplicate, then commented: "No sex discrimination here. We feel it is vital for everyone to know how to perform all these tasks. The girls gas cars. Mom takes it in for repairs. The boys cook and clean."

FAMILY PROJECTS

We also wondered if these effective families encouraged or created family projects, either to increase togetherness or to teach skills. We asked if their projects included gardening, doing genealogy, memorizing poetry or scriptures, building, remodeling, or adding on to the house; working in the family business; performing missionary activities; or being involved in service projects. The only projects that received a significant number of answers were:

1.	Family garden	74%
2.	Some service projects	58%
3.	Building or adding on to the home	48%
4.	Family business	47%

Forty-four families distributed their answers among the rest of the choices.

About three-fourths of the families had a garden, but it was not clear that all of the family members worked in the garden. Some families responded that the whole family helped prepare the plot and plant the seeds, but the up-keep fell on the mother or father or perhaps one child. A service project would often occur once or twice a year: taking a basket to a needy family for Christmas, helping a widow clean her yard, or doing something special for a family with an illness or some other special need.

MONEY

As discussed in chapter four in the section on motivation, 43 percent of the families use money as a reward for behavior they want to celebrate or encourage, but this figure was low compared to the 88 percent who use praise and the 72 percent who give permission to children to do something they particularly want.

Money in our society represents independence. It can come to people in two ways: as a gift motivated either by the recipient's need or the giver's generosity or as earned income, directly related to work.

ALLOWANCES

We asked our effective parents about allowances. Their responses showed clearly that there is no one right way to handle money in the family. Forty-three percent of the couples gave their children an allowance, but 57 percent did not. When we asked if the parents required their children to work for the money they gave them, the results were symmetrical. Nine percent said "always" and 9 percent said "never." Thirty-two percent said "most of the time," 13 percent said "often," 25 percent said "sometimes," and 12 percent said "seldom." Thus, equally effective families have very different strategies for dealing with money.

One Utah couple with five children ranging from three to sixteen had an allowance formula: "Twenty cents per week per year of age up to the age of ten. After that, the allowance is based on work completed around the home and yard." One couple gives each child a modest weekly allowance with a healthy bonus. For example, ten dollars a month if they follow the family guidelines on low-sugar use.

One father tied family money closely to the work ethic, explaining, "We have our children work for what they get. There are too many who grow up expecting things for nothing, and we think we can start at home to avoid this problem. If our children want money, they work for it." One Salt Lake City couple ruled, "Anyone who lived in the home was obligated to help keep it operating"; and when one daughter was going to summer school full time and could not hold a regular job, they paid her for yard work and cleaning the apartments they owned. "We feel this is wiser than giving her money," her mother wrote. "It becomes *her* money, and we have noticed that she spends it more judiciously."

At the other end of the spectrum, a father responded, "There are a lot of things more important than money, although it's certainly significant. We let our kids have what they need and don't require them to work for it per se. Working around the house is just part of being our family. We do for them what they need and hope that the advantages will pay off in the long run for them."

Among the families that gave allowances, many had set amounts for younger children but provided what was necessary to supplement what the teenagers earned on their own. The families paid weekly allowances in these ranges:

For ages 6-10
$1 a week	76%
$2 a week	14%
over $2 a week	10%

For ages 11-15
$1 a week	52%
$4 through $6	34%
$7 through $10	10%
over $10	4%

For ages 16-20
$1 through $5	57%
$6 through $10	21%
$11 through $20	16%
over $20	6%

Only fourteen families out of two hundred gave allowances to children twenty-one or older, and then the amounts varied widely. In one case where a daughter lived at home to care for an invalid parent, she received a sort of salary for her service to the family. Many parents also helped their college students by paying tuition and books or by providing room and board while the student worked part time. Some parents also gave a college student a car or helped pay for car expenses as a contribution toward education.

It is also clear from these results that the parents were not lavish with their children. Children under ten seldom received more than two dollars a week, and children under fifteen received about five dollars a week. Because many of these families usually do not allow dating before age sixteen, we expected to see an increase in allowance around that age; but even so, the weekly allowance was less than ten dollars a week. Many parents said that they provided money as needed for a trip, a special dress, or a prom; and an increasing number of children had part-time jobs of their own. In response to the question "Have your children obtained jobs outside the family while they were still living at home?", 94 percent responded yes; 4 percent responded no.

In some cases, these part-time jobs were seen as contributions to the family income, not as personal income. In other cases, the money belonged exclusively to the child. In one family, the father, a miner, was injured in an accident. "The kids just had to help with things," explained one of the married children. "Each one contributed so much of their babysitting money and then their wages, as they got older, and I don't think any of them regretted it. We all loved Dad so much and were happy to assist as we could. Now that some of us are married, it is a little easier to assist–since we make more money, and I know that Mom and Dad appreciate it."

Financial support from the children seemed to be the exception, however. Most of the comments from parents dealt instead with the thorny problem of allowances. Fifty-seven percent said something like: "No fixed allowances. We gave them what they needed." "We tried an allowance when the children were young," said one couple, "but found with us it was better to give money when they needed something. If they wanted something special, we gave special assignments and had them 'earn' their money. We kept track of their savings and payment of tithing. When they had 'savings', they could buy things. They would also add to their savings account at the credit union."

Another couple gave regular allowances and required

regular chores but said that their children were "allowed to work to earn extra money." Several families used this system. One mother wrote, "Occasionally, if extra money was needed, I would try to find a project—painting, extra yard or housework—that they could do for extra money. Allowances were given regardless of behavior or daily chores done."

One couple with four children wrote: "Our children have had an allowance, mainly to help them learn the principle of tithing and the principle of saving and managing money. When they needed money over and above what their allowance covered, we kept a list posted that included fifty-cent and dollar jobs. They could arrange with us how much extra work they wanted to do, after their regular chores were completed. We used a job chart when they were younger and assigned such chores as cleaning the bathroom and doing the dishes on a rotating basis. As they grew older, we sometimes made a list of jobs that needed doing and let them sign up for two or three they chose. Changing the method occasionally helped make the routine more interesting."

In some cases, payment was in kind. One farm couple did not try to keep track of how much work the children were required to do, but in exchange "they got a 4-H steer they sold for spending money, missions, and school." During busy times like the harvest, they also get wages. In an Idaho ranch family, the three children had to feed their calves before breakfast and catch the 7:30 a.m. bus. Both sons bought a dairy calf and a range calf from their father and received wages for taking care of the calves and also a percentage of the milk check. They could build their own herd as the animals matured, deciding whether to keep or sell their animals. The daughter also worked on the farm for wages. "She preferred it to housework," her mother commented.

In one Salt Lake City family, all ten children—seven sons and three daughters—had their own paper routes to earn spending money. When the parents needed babysitting, they would hire the older children to do it at one dollar an hour. They had set amounts for some jobs: five dollars to wash the car, five dollars to mow the lawn, five dollars a day for working in the father's accounting business, and so on.

For one couple, the most important value was teaching proper work habits to their children. Paraphrasing the Lord's commandment to Adam to "earn his living by the sweat of his brow," one couple explained: "We have taken it upon ourselves to teach this to our children. A lot of the problems of the world result from people who never learned to be dependable and to work. We go out of our way to find work for our children to do. It is not easy for us, as it was for our parents who lived on farms. When we were young, the jobs never ended; but here in the city, the jobs end sometimes. We scout out work for our children at home and in the neighborhood. There's always someone who is glad to get some yard work done. Our daughters all babysit. The jobs don't always just come. We sometimes have to help the children put signs and get the word out that they can babysit. This doesn't relieve them from their regular household duties. When time is short, the kids help each other, and we even help deliver newspapers when our son has to get through in a hurry to get to a special Scout program or something like that. Most of the time, we let him sweat it himself, however."

In a few families, money was not private property. One couple did not give allowances but allowed their children to earn spending money by doing yard work and babysitting when they reach the age ten or twelve. "We function under the idea that since we work as a family, all the money that comes in is for all of the family. The children ask for money when they have a need; if the money is available, they receive the amount needed.

One Utah family with nine children and a disabled father used a "United Order" model. All the money that came in belonged to the whole family. This common fund "paid the bills, sent missionaries, and so on," wrote the mother. "When they needed anything, and if it was a good thing and if it was possible to give it to them, they got it." She praised their financial management: "They do not spend money foolishly. They can have money in their pocket and never spend it if they don't need to."

In one Idaho family with twenty-one children from four marriages, each child celebrated his sixteenth birthday by being placed on the family checking account. He or she could then draw from it with permission.

Still another couple accustomed their eight children to the world of work by paying an hourly wage. With a Montana farm, they found it comparatively simple to work out a regular bookkeeping system: "The children get money only when they work. Up to age ten they earn between a dollar and three dollars an hour. Up to fifteen, they make between two and three-fifty an hour. Between sixteen and twenty, they earn three to four-fifty an hour, and more during harvest—up to eighty dollars a day. Over twenty-one, they earn between four and eight dollars an hour, and they put in long hours." This couple also pointed out that their children are very good at saving most of their summer wages and that the four boys old enough for missions have paid at least half of their own way.

SUPPORT FOR MARRIED CHILDREN

We were also interested to know how the financial arrangements within families changed for married children. Is providing money in a different category than supplying emotional support, child care, and other goods or services? It would be interesting to have comparative national statistics, but the best available are from a 1983 *Better Homes & Gardens* survey called "What's Happening to American Families?" This survey showed that 56 percent of the parents surveyed would let a married child return home to live for a limited time, 21 percent would welcome an adult child back with no reservations, 9 percent would be reluctant, and 6 percent would refuse. Most family experts generally believe that many parents supply money or child-care service for their young married children and also supply money and care for *their* elderly parents. In our sample, 14 percent of the parents tended grandchildren regularly for married children who worked, and an additional 60 percent tended grandchildren occasionally. Sixty-four percent "gave advice" to their married children, 52 percent gave money as gifts, and 50 percent loaned money to married children. We were pleased to see that 60 percent of the fathers gave blessings to their married children on request.

As usual, the comments added to this section were illuminating. A Utah couple with fourteen children helped their four married children build or remodel their homes. Several couples mentioned supplying food to their married children, particularly meat and milk from dairy farms and cattle ranches, fresh fruit and garden produce, bottled fruit, and food-storage items. Car repairs and the loan of a vehicle were also mentioned. A Salt Lake mother made home-sewn clothing for her six children and twelve grandchildren. One Wyoming couple has co-signed notes with their two married children.

An Idaho couple have a family partnership on their farm with their two sons. One son and his family live in the basement apartment where the parents lived as newlyweds. "The partnership makes things somewhat equal," the father wrote. "The farm has paid for everyone's schooling, missions for both sons and our daughter, and [provides] individual pay as a living wage every month. Our arrangement is probably unusual. Everyone must work, but we all work together and share, and we consider one another's well-being. We work hard at getting along, too, especially by letting our children discipline and raise their own children."

One Utah couple owns a fourplex and have allowed all of their children to live in it rent free at one time or another, "While they were finishing the last year of school or when they were newly married." Still another Utah couple has an "open-door policy on our food-storage in the basement when our married children are hard up." A Salt Lake couple gives each child a quarter-acre of land when he or she marries. Each may choose to build on it or sell. Still another Salt Lake City couple usually gives each newlywed couple "a piece or two of furniture from our home."

While all of these effective families have worked out some system for channeling money to their children, they usually do not buy good behavior with it. Parents give money as it is needed, will pay for work, or will give an allowance because the children are "part of the family." There seems to be a common feeling that money is either shared or earned.

None of the parents in our study indicated that money for the children was a particularly difficult problem. Many did what seemed appropriate at the time, changing their strategy as the times, needs, and children changed. One couple wrote: "As with so many other areas, we have tried a lot of different things. One thing worked for one child and another for another. We don't see how some parents set up one system and hold to that as if it were the only way. If we had done that, we couldn't have made allowances a helpful system in dealing with our children. Money is a tool, not the master; *whom* the money is given to is a tool, too, not a master.

NURTURING THE HUSBAND-WIFE RELATIONSHIP

Although this study focused on parenting in effective families, it is impossible not to consider the effect of the husband-wife relationship on the ability to provide love and direction to the children. The well-known words of President David O. McKay to fathers come to mind. "The best thing you can do for your children is to love their mother."

As we interviewed the less-effective families, several of them indicated problems in their marriage as well as dissatisfaction with their parenting. "We do not have what I would call a special family," said one woman sadly. "In almost every way we have botched it. Our family fights a lot, and the marriage has about come apart for a number of reasons. I doubt we could do any better if we were going to begin again with a fresh start. Nobody taught us to be parents, and I guess we didn't get it from instinct."

Another wife also expressed the same sense of near hopelessness: "Finances have been tough for a long time, and we fight about it a lot. My husband works all the time and is never home much. Things aren't too happy for us."

One couple actually divorced, then remarried. "We try harder, but it doesn't always work out," they said. The wife wrote that one of the best things they had going for them was their "strong determination to lead a fairly happy life in spite of major differences in husband and wife." Another woman admitted, "It's hard to get the children to understand that marriage is really important when I have been divorced two times."

For some, all marital satisfaction was almost completely gone. One woman observed flatly, "My husband hasn't told me that he loves me since we were married, over twenty years ago." A husband admitted, "I just got some time on my hands, and started seeing this other woman, and one thing led to another, and everything just sort of fell apart."

No marriage is trouble free. The highly effective couples in our study are the last to claim any special exemption from problems, but they seem to have found out how to keep a high-quality, committed relationship as husband and wife. As one wife said: "We are so pleased that we were raised when couples worked out their problems instead of giving up the marriage, as so many now do. This is one thing that we have really talked about with our children. No marriage is perfect, but it becomes more so as problems are worked out with love and understanding. After all, this earth life is to build both [for] here and for eternal worlds. Good families move right into the next life."

We asked each couple several questions about household chores, decisions, and general happiness:

1. In your present family, who usually does each of these tasks:

Earns family income?
Does the housekeeping?
Keeps in touch with relatives?
Organizes family recreation?
Cares for preschool children?
Teaches, helps, and disciplines girls ages 6-12?
Teaches, helps, and disciplines boys ages 6-12?

2. Who makes most of the decisions about:
Earning family income?
Doing the housekeeping?
Keeping in touch with relatives?
Family recreation?
Sexual intimacy?
Duties and behavior of girls ages 6-12?
Duties and behavior of boys ages 6-12?

We asked them to check one of five choices: husband entirely, husband more, both equally, wife more, wife entirely.

3. All things considered, please indicate the degree of happiness of your marriage by marking an x on the following scale:

Very happy		Very unhappy
marriage	9 8 7 6 5 4 3 2 1	marriage

The parents in the sample responded this way:

Scale Number	Percent
3	2%

5	2%
6	2%
7	8%
8	16%
9	71%

The average score for all of the families was 8.5, a good indication of the happiness in their marriages. Nearly three-fourths of the parents felt their marriage was a 9. One Washington man and his second wife (his first had died) had been married for about eight years when they took this survey. The wife circled 9 and drew sunbeams around it, adding, "We feel that our marriage is very rewarding to us. We are best friends." One national survey with a similar scale showed 20 percent of the couples reporting "unhappy" marriages while the rest were "relatively happy" (Leslie Gerald, *The Family in Social Context* [New York: Oxford, 1979]). In a 1983 study of 200,000 people, 81 percent of the married respondents would marry their present spouse if they had it all to do over again, and 79 percent indicated that their "expectations of happiness are being fulfilled." (*Better Homes and Gardens*, "What's Happening to American Families?" [New York: Meredith Corporation, 1983].)

It is logical to suspect a certain bias in the response to this question. These parents knew they were part of a study that was looking at good LDS families, and they may have felt some pressure to indicate they felt their marriage was a happy one. Still, 30 percent marked below the highest score, indicating some areas of disturbance. And 4 percent placed themselves at the midpoint or lower.

We can draw two inferences from these scores. On one

hand, it would seem that effective families are led by parents who have a very positive feeling about the happiness of their marriage. On the other hand, it seems possible in some cases, to have a family that the stake president and others regard as highly effective even if the marriage is less than ideally happy. Very few people wrote comments about the marital score itself, but one wife commented that the financial worries were their chief problem, with sexual incompatibility next. Another wife indicated a lower happiness score than her husband and penciled in: "It's that darn money!"

None of the families we interviewed would say they have a perfect marriage, and all admitted to having had real problems and adjustments as they have lived together. They have had personality differences. One spouse wanted to talk things out, the other didn't. Expectations about how to run a home or rear children have differed. But through it all, the couples have had a common set of goals and values and a desire to stay together and be a happy family.

What are some patterns that contribute to harmony or to dissatisfaction? This table shows how the husbands and wives in these families divide up certain tasks.

Task	Husband Entirely	Husband More	Equal	Wife Entirely	Wife More
Earns family income	62%	34%	3%	.5%	.5%
Housekeeping	1%	3%	70%	26%	
Keeps in touch with relatives	3%	37%	54%	6%	
Organizes family recreation	9%	58%	31%	2%	
Cares for pre

school children		10%	77%	13%
Teaches, helps, and disciplines girls ages 6-12	3%	52%	44%	1%
Teaches, helps, and disciplines boys ages 6-12	8%	56%	35%	1%

In this table, the only duty listed as clearly the domain of the father is earning the family income, while the mother is clearly responsible for keeping up the house and taking care of the preschool children. This is a predictable pattern in couples of this particular generation and matches what we learned about Americans in general from national data.

The mother's rather exclusive responsibility for preschoolers shifts once the children enter school. The parents reported that more than 50 percent of the fathers worked with children of both sexes ages six to twelve.

Husbands sometimes took the responsibility for planning family recreation, although they were likely to share this task equally with their wives. One wife remarked wryly, "My husband plans a lot of his own recreation but not much for the whole family." However, another husband, reflecting on the general topic of division of labor, wrote: "It takes a lot of effort to make money for the family to obtain the things my wife and I have decided are important. She doesn't work outside the home, but believe me, she works hard—I think much harder than I do. Her work is really never done. I try to help with the children and with things in the home all I can, but admittedly, most if it falls to her. I love her for what she does, and someday perhaps I will be able to do more. It makes me feel bad when I see how some of the husbands I know try to get out of helping their wives by staying away, or going on a lot of fishing trips. Women are pretty special to do so much and complain so little."

As the data on household chores reveals, most parents taught both sons and daughters to do most tasks, although boys were more commonly assigned to working in the yard, repairing cars, garden or field work, and dealing with ranch animals, while girls were more likely to be cooking, housecleaning, and doing dishes. It is expected that these same patterns would hold for mother and father. It would be interesting to discover, in view of the national trends toward more egalitarian marriages, if this parental pattern is modified in their children's families.

After asking about the breakdown of tasks, we asked how decisions were made in the following areas.

Decision	Husband Entirely	Husband More	Equal	Wife Entirely	Wife More
Earns family income	28%	52%	21%		
Housekeeping		1%	7%	66%	26%
Keeps in touch with relatives		2%	52%	42%	4%
Family recreation		8%	75%	17%	1%
Sexual intimacy	2%	28%	65%	5%	
Duties of girls ages 6-12			52%	46%	1%
Duties of boys ages 6-12		18%	58%	23%	1%

Comparing responses, we see a general parallel between parents and children, but it is clear that many couples make joint decisions even though only one will actually perform the task. For example, even though earning the family income is predominantly the husband's task, 21 percent said the wives have an equal voice in making decisions about their husband's work. One wife explained: "My husband and I talk over every decision he makes about his work. In the past we have jointly decided not to take a promotion that meant moving the family. We have resisted work assignments that interfered with Sunday activities or family vacations. I feel I should have a say in those kinds of work decisions that affect the family." One Utah couple, the husband in his early fifties and the wife in her mid-forties, described a traditional relationship that seems to work in a very egalitarian way: "We have a patriarch in our home who loves the Lord and is committed to obeying his commandments, including teaching our four children. He is also willing to accept and implement suggestions from me. We work well as a family presidency and have regular meetings to plan for the family."

Several couples expressed strong feelings on the subject of marital unity. One Utah couple in their mid-forties with five children wrote that "husband-wife unity—a strong relationship through thick and thin!" was one of the most important factors in making them a strong family. Another Utah couple with nine children, ages seven to twenty-two reported: "We, as marriage partners, are in love and are absolutely committed to each other. As parents we are absolutely committed to the gospel. We work hard at teaching our children what is right and at helping to channel them, but we respect their free agency." One Washington wife wrote: "We feel that because we, as husband and wife, have a great feeling of love and respect for one another and a very rewarding relationship, that this will set an example for our children and help them to have happy marriages. Our one married child has a happy marriage."

A Utah couple with nine children ranging from ages nine to twenty-four observed, "We feel a sense of security in the concept 'Love is harmony even in discord.'" An Idaho couple strongly believed in "sticking together on discipline, whether they agreed at the time or not."

In another Utah family, also perceived as highly effective, the parents acknowledged strong differences between them. The husband commented, "Our compatibility has grown somewhat less as my wife's education has increased. However, we have tried to keep our differences from our seven children." They had marked two places on the marital happiness scale, the wife about an 8 and the husband about a 7. At other points in the survey they had written their own answers when they differed from each other. For instance, the husband felt that the most important factor in the family's success was "going to church together," while the wife felt that it was "letting our children know—no matter what—that we really love them." The husband feels that the children "must do" all of the activities they checked, while the wife "doesn't like the term 'must.'" They also rated their preferred discipline styles differently. Obviously, they were able to acknowledge and deal with these differences, and not feel that the differences paralyzed the marriage or had to be concealed.

We added the issue of the couple's sexual intimacy because this is a much-studied area nationally. With 65 percent of these couples, decisions about intimacy seem to be shared. In 28 percent of the cases, the husband was seen as more influential in these decisions. (Nationally, 80 percent of both spouses indicated that sexual activity is initiated by the husband. [F. Ivan Nye, *Role Structure and Analysis of the Family* (Beverly Hills, Calif.: Sage Publications), p. 105.] Two percent indicated that the husband was completely responsible for decisions about intimacy. We do not have data to determine if this is acceptable to the wife or whether it is a point of disturbance in the relationship. Our data also show that in 5 percent of the cases, decisions about intimacy are primarily the responsibility of the wife. Again our data do not show if the wife's decision is to initiate or resist intimacy.

As we would expect from couples of this generation, they consider sexual intimacy to be a personal and private matter, not one to be discussed openly. Respecting these feelings, we did not probe deeply during the follow-up interviews. One couple shared this appraisal: "We have found that our sex life has undergone a lot of changes through the years. Early in our marriage there was concern about pregnancies, and we never completely resolved our feelings about using birth control methods. There was often a difference in the eagerness and energy we had toward responding to each other. The wife was often tired from a lot of work with a lot of children and outside assignments. It seemed that for a time she would go along to meet the needs of the husband. As children have gone from the home and we have fewer pressures, our own relationship has become more important and more satisfying, although there is still some imbalance in terms of who has the stronger needs."

Sexual incompatibility is often cited by non-professionals as a "cause" of divorce, but statistics show very little correlation between marital happiness and sexual satisfaction. (Randall Collins, *Sociology of Marriage and the Family* [Chicago: Prentice-Hall, 1985], p. 249.) However, it is probably true that sexual problems are symptomatic of other problems. Couples who are angry over money problems or exhausted by fights with their teenagers may use the sexual relationship as a weapon in fighting about their differences.

Many of the couples in the survey would probably agree with one couple's analysis of their own compatibility: "Our answers to these questions as to how happy our marriage is and how various decisions are made will vary depending on such things as stress, pressures, mood, cycles, and health." Other families have indicated that while they have a generally consistent pattern of making decisions, shifts and variations in circumstances will cause "periodic readjustments and fluctuations."

A Utah couple in their mid-sixties with seven children wrote, "Our family has been our top priority. As parents we have desired some individuality too, not just living for our children. We have felt that the things we pursued together as a family have been important—additional education, cultural refinement, missions, civic and church involvement. All of these things have enhanced our children's involvement."

For another couple, the key to successful parenting is that "there was always unity between husband and wife. We shared Church positions, welfare assignments, and meetings. Our children also shared in all of these things because it was part of family life." A Wyoming couple in their early fifties, the youngest of their six children now eighteen, agreed that the most important factor in making a strong family was "acting together as husband and wife, as mother and father, and always keeping a strong front."

The high commitment to gospel ideals and the deliberate, long-term cultivation of love in the home that nearly all of these effective couples have achieved, are both signs that the husband and wife closely shared the same interests and goals. It is true that couples with similar goals and values have happier, less stressful marriages. Many years ago, a popular notion was that "opposites attract," and that differences make a marriage more interesting. However, enough inevitable differences exist in most marriages that it is unnecessary to advise a couple to look for more. One couple wrote: "We used to have more problems in our marriage than we do now. We never really had too many serious problems, just the little things that come along now and again. Well, they don't come along so much anymore, and we would say that we have never been happier in our marriage. We started out happy, and things have really just gotten better all the time. We thought we were happy then, but we are happier now. We have always thought that we couldn't be happier, but each year gets better, especially as the children have gotten older."

These effective couples have highly compatible values. They want the same things for their children—missions, temple marriage, education, strong family ties. They have been willing to spend their time and money on the family. They have generally had large families and have devoted a great deal of time to teaching them, and modeling Church teachings for them. They have spent a lot of time talking with and teaching their children.

It has been their goal to rear a good family, to prepare as much as they could to be a family that might be a candidate for celestial heritage. All of these families acknowledged certain weaknesses and shortcomings. But the essence of their lives is clearly that they have tried to live as close as they can to the standards and values they believe in. They want to be a close, unified family. One couple wrote: "We fell in love a long time ago and made the commitment to team up in this life. Some of the time we had difficulties, but we have worked at it, and we think we love each other more as the years go by. Some of the hardest times were when most of the children were starting to get older, but we stuck it out. We really do love each other, and our children sense that. We talk and share. We pray together and do a lot of planning about our family. We think the Lord helps us a lot in our marriage and with our kids."

An almost mirror reversal of this position is the statement of a husband in one of the less-effective families: "We have had our share of problems as a family. My wife and I have not been able to get along like we should always. Some of our kids have acted out and this has brought us a lot of embarrassment. I see a lot of families who seem to have things together, and how I wish we could be more like them. I don't know, I guess we made our bed and now we have to sleep in it. All of my sisters' families do well, and my wife's brothers and sisters do well too, but we just have had a hard time. I guess we love each other, but most of the time it doesn't get demonstrated very well."

Which comes first? A good marriage or good parenting? It's probably impossible to decide. But when parents are truly committed to family-centered goals, they seem happy together in their marriages and feel that what they are accomplishing is good. The sense of contentment they feel is real.

CHAPTER NINE

KEY 9

DEALING WITH ADVERSITY

We learned from our interviews and personal observations that all families have trials and problems, and we wondered: "What do strong families do when adversity strikes?" Do problems and difficulties divide or strengthen families?

We asked each couple these four questions:

1. Has your family ever encountered any real family problems or adversities?
2. If so, what were they?
3. How long did they last?
4. How did you handle them?

We wanted to probe what constituted adversity for these families and what their coping mechanisms were. The evidence indicates that even though the families experienced difficulties, they were able to cope with them; and, as many families indicated, the problems strengthened them.

To the question, "Have you experienced any real family problems or adversities?" about 20 percent answered "no." Thirty percent said they had experienced several severe problems, and the other 50 percent were in between—they had experienced some real problems, but not what they considered to be an unusual number of them.

These percentages are probably on the low side. During our follow-up interviews, we found that some couples who had marked "no real problems" had, in fact, faced a number of problems, including long-term unemployment, illnesses, and disappointments with children. However, they had compared themselves to others who had suffered the death of a child or permanent disability of a family member and felt that their problems were relatively insignificant. One couple told us: "We have had problems, but we just never thought of them as special problems. If illness, death, and financial problems are problems, we have had them. But Job suffered more, and we think that one purpose of this life is to encounter problems, so we certainly wouldn't single ourselves out as anything special on this account. It's true that many whom we know seem to have clearer sailing in this life. Perhaps the Lord will test them in some other manner."

Another husband offered an explanation: "We have had a number of family problems in our married life. I have had a heart attack, but recovered. We have had to take care of aged parents for many years. My wife's brothers and sisters have had divorces and problems. But in our own family, we have been blessed. Our boys have all filled missions. Our daughter married a fine young man in the temple. Compared to other families we know, we really have never had any real problems."

Among the families who were willing to define their problems as adversities, the following difficulties were listed:

1. Health problems (illness, disabilities, accidents)   40%
2. A rebellious or problem child   19%
3. Death of family member(s)   15%
4. Business of financial reversals   14%
5. Word of Wisdom problems (drugs, alcohol, etc.)   4%
6. Divorce   3%
7. Fire or other natural disasters   3%

National measures of family stress usually turn up the same problems: divorce, death, drugs, alcohol, abuse, unemployment, and so on. The families in our survey clearly define health problems as the major difficulty they have had to face. An interesting note is that to some extent, illness and accidents are outside the control of individuals. People do not "decide" to be sick or healthy. The second greatest problem, having a rebellious child, is a matter of someone's will. The child decides to depart from the family norms and values.

These good families are not problem free. They have drunk from the bitter cup, but they seem to have been able to cope with these problems, not be devastated by them. When we asked how long they had suffered from these adversities, 63 percent responded that they had faced the situations for years, and another 24 percent indicated the problems had lasted for many months. Several people who suffered deaths in the family wrote comments like, "When is a death 'over'?" These problems, in other words, are not short-term matters.

In response to the question about how they handled their adversity, about 35 percent of the couples said that they had turned to the Lord in prayer, fasting, and exercising their faith. About an equal number (30 percent) described a process of accepting the situation, developing patience, and assuming the burden of living successfully with the adversity. ("We lived through it," was a stoical comment that appeared more than once.)

Another group (22 percent) said that the family had pulled together and strengthened each other so they could deal with the situation, whether it involved finding a solution to the problem, or developing the patience to live with it. One Texas couple with six children had suffered illnesses, the death of loved ones, and financial difficulties. "We handled them one day at a time," they explained. "Fasting, prayer, and the support of each other all helped."

More than seventy-five of the 200 families explained their problems in enough detail that we could glimpse both their dimensions and their solutions.

In one Utah family with nine children, the husband was disabled and ill during most of the years the children were growing up. For a good many years, he was confined to a wheelchair and threatened with the loss of his legs. His inability to work and provide for his family was a secondary but very real problem. His wife wrote, "We try to make our problems pay off for us by being thankful for our added time together and looking at the positive side of problems." Among those positive aspects were the children's learning to rely on the Spirit, and the unity fostered by working for the common good. The children have also always contributed their income to a common fund.

A Texas couple with four children endured illnesses and

broken bones among the children, and the much more disruptive illnesses of the parents—open-heart surgery for the father, thyroid surgery for the mother. "Self-reliance and...an eternal perspective have helped," they wrote. "Prayers are important and very strengthening to all of us."

A Utah couple recalled as their greatest times of trouble, a terrifying two-week crisis when they almost lost one of their eight children to spinal meningitis, and a longer crisis when their eldest daughter ran away at sixteen. "That crisis lasted six months—maybe it isn't completely over yet," wrote the mother. They had dealt with the first crisis with "lots of prayer and communicating" for emotional support. They used the same method in trying to reach their daughter again. "Professional counseling also helped," she added.

With "faith in the gospel and much prayer, we made it through," wrote a Montana farm couple with five living children. A sixth had died and another has Down's syndrome. Drought and hail had decimated their crops, and various accidents around the farm had been debilitating to other members of the family.

A Utah couple with eight children had one child who required open-heart surgery, brain surgery, and numerous hospital stays. Another child involved in a car accident was hospitalized for a long time and required eye surgery, physical therapy, occupational therapy, and special schools. The family finances suffered, and the mother fought recurring bouts of depression. "We handled it by dropping everything else and just carrying on," wrote the father.

A young daughter in one family developed cystic fibrosis. "Everyone knew that this was a terminal disease," reported the father. "All of the children, both older and younger, treated this little girl with special care. She was a beautiful, loving child. You couldn't help but love her. But she was the one that everyone tried to help, be with, or do for."

One Idaho farmer, now seventy-eight, lost his first wife when she died at age thirty-one, leaving five children. Their first child together died. His second wife bore eight children in ten years and died at age thirty-four. A third marriage, which produced five surviving children (two babies who died soon after birth), again ended with the death of his wife at age fifty. His fourth wife brought eight children to the marriage. He also laconically listed "several serious accidents, crop failures, etc." among his moments of adversity, commenting that "they lasted from one to the next." In answer to the question about how he handled the hardships, his wife wrote: "1 Nephi 3:7." That scripture reads, "I will go and do the things which the Lord hath commanded, for I know that the Lord giveth no commandments unto the children of men, save he shall prepare a way for them that they may accomplish the thing which he commandeth them."

For twenty of their almost thirty-year marriage, one Idaho couple coped with their particular adversity: Their second child was killed at the age of ten in a sleighing accident. Her younger brother became handicapped and died at age nineteen. All four grandparents died. "Being close together is the way we gained strength," they wrote.

A Wyoming couple with five children stoically listed "death of a baby, home fire, cancer and the loss of Mother's leg, health and surgery, and taking over the family ranch" among their adversities, handled by "prayer, fasting, and blessings, and a lot of family communication."

One Washington family underwent the strain of losing their mother when the four children were between the ages of five and twelve. The second marriage added two children to the family and readjustments to all over the next fifteen years. The parents wrote: "One boy acted out a great deal of anger, but loves his family. A healing still needs to take place with all the older children in regard to their mother's death. They all have some anger and will not attend church now; however, they are very responsible and independent people. The grief gets better with time, but it will never end. There is always an empty spot for Mom. It's a challenge to build and maintain unity; but we love the gospel and our children. We've experienced times when only our faith in God gave us hope and encouragement. We have seen miracles take place in seemingly simple ways and feel that we have great blessings."

One Texas couple with five children suffered deeply when their oldest daughter went through three or four years of flouting family standards, finally giving birth to a child out of wedlock. "We try to be there when she needs us," they explained, "but we want her to be responsible. We backed off on giving advice and we also backed off on giving help. We have not helped financially with the baby."

One Utah management consultant had to work abroad for a year, a time that his wife acknowledged as a strain. All of their seven children who were old enough graduated from seminary; the boys who were old enough served missions. One daughter did not marry in the temple, however, and the wife felt that dealing with this "child who wouldn't follow counsel" had been a source of adversity that they had handled "with much prayer and fasting, and relying on the

Spirit". "On occasion," she added, "we have sought counsel from professionals in the problem area—usually someone we knew already who advised us about specific problems."

A Texas couple with five children recalled concern over the poor grades of one child and the troubled marriage of an older daughter. "In both cases," they wrote, "we got professional evaluation and counseling, and we gave our personal advice and support."

A Montana couple were grieved when three of their six children had "morality problems," but the problems did not last long and all three went to the bishop on their own.

A Texas couple with five children were saddened by the long-term inactivity of their oldest child. "He has since returned" they reported. They describe themselves as "a very affectionate family". "We love each other and tell it often." Thus, it was especially painful when their oldest daughter's in-laws misunderstood her, creating a problem that lasted about two years. "Fasting, prayer, and love is how we handled both problems," wrote the mother.

A Montana couple with seven children had one son who "found himself in serious trouble with the authorities." During the three-month ordeal, they tried to keep their problem in perspective: "Every family has its share of crummy happenings. You handle them with prayer, love, and support for whoever needs it." The lesson they learned was "bending with the adversity so as not to break," but still, they confessed, "it's awfully hard, putting away wonderful beautiful dreams about a child's life and just standing behind him, loving him no matter what."

A California couple with four children suffered the loss of their third child, which tragedy "brought the family even closer," they wrote. "We all want to be worthy to be with her again." Another problem was that the parents had a strong preference about which college one daughter should go to. They reported candidly, "She obeyed her father but hated it, so we let her go to her choice and it worked out fine. She was right, and we admitted it." Another couple, grieved when their son came home from his mission early, found all the family "pulling more together and relying on the Lord." The son in one Idaho family accepted a mission call then eloped. A daughter was diagnosed as having cancer, and the father nearly died from health problems that resulted in twenty days of hospitalization and six months of recuperation. "Prayer and family councils were our mainstay," wrote the mother.

In another Utah family with three children, a classic but hardly reassuring pattern of teenage rebellion, drug abuse, and dishonesty occurred. The parents handled it "first with confrontation, then more with patience, prayer, and understanding." An Idaho couple with five children had a problem for about a year with one teenager's "improper reading materials, Word of Wisdom temptations, and spending habits." They handled the situation by "expressing our disappointment and explaining the hazards, then demonstrating increased love."

A Utah couple with five children struggled for twelve years with their rebellious eldest son who dropped out of school, stole, and was abusive to the other children. They worked with a counselor and their bishop, and resorted to foster placement for a month. They have seen him gradually return to Church activity, family relationships, and school. Another couple with six children are still living in a nightmare that followed their eighteen-year-old son's alleged homosexual rape. "We thought he was okay—just scared," they wrote. "Now he says he's homosexual, has rejected all authority, and has turned to homosexual friends."

Several parents mentioned, as a source of adversity, the negative influence of friends. A Utah couple with eight living children underwent a two-year period of seeing their children influenced adversely by friends. Their method of dealing with the problem was using "logic and encouraging new friends." One Montana couple with four children saw their eldest daughter begin dating nonmembers and, after six months, marry one. A Montana couple had one daughter marry out of the temple and later divorce, as did her sister who had been married in the temple. This sister also had experimented with drinking and smoking. In answer to the question, "How did you handle these adversities?" the parents wrote from the heart. "We feel really bad."

In one Utah family, the couple had married in the temple when they were both in their early twenties. The husband is a university professor, and his long schooling was a financial struggle for the family, particularly because the first three of their five children were born within the first five years of their marriage. Also, the wife had had difficult pregnancies. They faced their problems with "work, prayer, fasting, faith, and endurance."

A Utah couple with eight children weathered a ten-year financial crisis coupled with the serious four-year illness of one family member by "pooling all our resources, including our talents, to deal with it." Adversity made them "more considerate, helpful, and prayerful," they wrote. A Utah couple with seven children identified as their chief problem the financial difficulties caused by the husband's unsatisfactory employment. (He is currently a janitor.) "We endured job changes again and again for twenty-three years," the wife wrote. This couple rated their marital happiness at about an 8, and the wife jotted down: "Financial worries are the main problem" followed by sexual differences. (They had indicated that decisions about sexual intimacy were equally shared.)

For another couple, adversities include the financial difficulties of a son who struggled to pay school debts and support his family. This couple has given and loaned money, and provided occasional child care, advice, and blessings to all their married children. They comment, "Our son is still having money problems, but he's working them out. We helped some but feel he should handle it himself."

A Salt Lake City couple suffered severe financial reversals when the husband's partners embezzled from the firm. "Prayer, hard work, and being positive about the future" were chief strategies for handling these problems. An Idaho farm equipment manager with ten children found himself in serious financial difficulty when his partner pulled out, leaving them with all the debts to pay. He and his wife negotiated with the debtors and, over a five-year period, "paid off the obligations and cleared our name." Another Idaho couple was forced to change their financial future when the bank foreclosed on their business. The husband had at age forty-eight to find a new occupation. They had already weathered the wife's three-year disability and had managed, they felt, "very well."

An Idaho couple felt that their most serious problem was gradually being forced to realize that they could not make a living at farming, especially when the third of their eight children was injured and permanently handicapped.

After a three-year struggle, they sold the farm and went back to school, and both became teachers.

An Idaho family survived the year-long recuperation of a child scalded so badly that hospitalization was required for two months. It took them three years to get back on their feet when their home was destroyed in the 1976 Teton Dam flood in southeastern Idaho. During both traumatic periods, they relied on "blessings, the psychological support of friends and family, keeping busy with hard work, and planning ahead even when there seemed to be no future. "

Other types of problems also showed up on the questionnaire. One Utah couple with seven children had a baby die, but the adversity they listed was overcome by "getting along, considering one another's feelings, overcoming selfishness and impatience." A Utah couple with four children experienced as their greatest trial one period when the husband had to work out of state for extended periods of time. "Thank goodness that only lasted a few months," wrote the wife, "and we got through with lots of prayer and fasting and our patriarchal blessings." One Texas couple mentioned marital problems as adversity, but added that "prayer, work, and faith had resolved them after a few weeks."

Only two couples said they had handled their problems "well". Conversely, only two or three said they handled them "not too well." Thus, most of the families feel that they *have* handled their difficulties. To a remarkable degree, they also seem to have handled them as internal problems and with internal resources. It is interesting to note that with all of the problems with health, not more than half a dozen families mentioned doctors as sources of help in coping with their problems, even though their technical assistance goes without saying. Approximately a dozen gave credit to counselors or therapists for helping with emotional problems. About the same number mentioned bishops or other Church authorities. No doubt, some families consulted professional people and their bishops, as in the case of medical assistance, but apparently the coping process inside the family was not noticeably influenced by these professionals. Prayer, blessings, and fasting were often mentioned. The *Better Homes and Gardens* survey asked couples to identify whom they turned to for help in confronting significant problems. Seventy-one percent reported that they turned to the family, 21 percent to friends, 10 percent to clergy, 7 percent to another member of their church, 2 percent to a co-worker, and 7 percent to "other." Thus, the family-centeredness of the effective families in our survey is emphasized by this comparison.

It is probably impossible to determine which came first—strength to handle adversity well or the adversity that produced increased strength. Certainly, working through their problems made these families stronger, no matter the comparative strengths with which they began. Also, the feeling of success in coping with their problems would no doubt have increased their ability to deal with other forms of stress.

One couple quoted Ether 12:27 in an interview: "If men come unto me I will show unto them their weakness that they may be humble; and my grace is sufficient for all men that humble themselves before me; for if they humble themselves before me, and have faith in me, then will I make weak things become strong unto them." They commented, "We think this is how working out problems happens in our family. For us, this scripture explains how the Lord uses problems to help people make something out of life."

The findings in this area of the study surprised us. Since these are strong, active Church-going families, we thought they would mention the Church as a major element in coping with adversity. But the number of people who mentioned a bishop, a quorum leader, a home or visiting teacher was small. We found that faith in the Lord, fasting and prayer were deeply important. The family was the first line of defense. Church members and programs were a secondary, although important, source of support.

DEVELOPING SUPPORTIVE RELATIONSHIPS

At the start of our research, part of our hypothesis was that effective families could not just turn inward and ignore the outside world. In proving this, we wanted to know who the children played with, who were their peer groups and who were their heroes.

We asked questions to get some insight into how friends and older siblings influenced children, and whether heroes outside the family had much impact. The questions were as follows:

1. Please indicate for your children how many friends they had compared with most other children their age. (Following their question was a grid with the number of children and the choices of "more friends," "the same number," and "fewer friends.")
2. Our children's friends...

____have been a very helpful influence for our children.

____have seldom been of value in our children's lives.

____have frequently led our children astray.

3. When your children are with their friends, do they spend the time

____mostly in the homes of the friends?

____about equally in each home?

____mostly in your home?

4. Do you approve of your children's friends

____most of the time?

____sometimes?

____almost never?

5. How important do you think your older children are in shaping the younger children?

____very important

____somewhat important

____not too important

____not at all important

6. If your older children help shape the younger ones, how do they do this? (Following were the choices of showing an example, helping with school lessons, encouraging the younger ones to study or work hard, preparing talks, writing encouraging letters, attending functions where the young ones are participating, and "other.")

7. Do you have any heroes as a family? If so, who are they?

FRIENDS

Eighty-five percent of the families in the survey indicated that the children's friends have been a "very helpful" influence. One couple checked that answer on their questionnaire but also reported that one daughter had married a good but inactive man while another daughter's first marriage, which ended in divorce, had not been a temple marriage.

The number of friends seemed to be related to age. Only 22 percent of first-born children had more friends than most of the other children in the family who had "more than most." Furthermore, between 15 and 20 percent of the families felt that their children as a whole had fewer friends than most. In some cases, this perception may have simply reflected the fact that there were plenty of children at home to play with and that the family's emphasis on unity would tend to draw children and their friends into the family rather than encouraging the children to seek companionship elsewhere.

A few parents expressed concern that a particular child did not have more friends. One couple wrote: "We always worried about our third child. He seemed to have a hard time making friends and always spent a lot of time doing things alone. We tried to invite children in and foster friendships, but it never was easy. Our other children all seemed to make friends easily and had lots of companions. It was hard for us to see this child left out when others were going places with their friends." However, another couple said, "Our youngest son didn't have very many friends, but he did have one or two with whom he was very close. This seemed to satisfy his friendship needs, so we didn't worry too much because these close friends were good boys and had a good influence on him." A Texas couple with seven children took the long view in pointing out that their second son had only one friend all through high school, "but now that he's in college he has many and is more open and lively."

Thirteen percent of the parents felt that some of their children's friends had "seldom" been a positive influence, and 2 percent felt that some of these friends had been downright negative in leading their children away from family norms. One Utah couple with five children checked the "very helpful" box but wrote, "Friends led one child astray temporarily." A second Utah couple with six children also checked the "very helpful" box but qualified their answer. "One child had problems for a period of time with friends we would not have chosen." An Idaho couple wrote that friends have "sometimes" been of value in their children's lives. They explained, "There are some exceptions; but generally they have had to learn to stand up for their own convictions."

One father denied any significant impact from friends by observing, "Our children's friends have been of great value to them but have not influenced their basic values—either for good or for bad." One Montana couple who checked "seldom" observed, "We live in a very small branch, and most of the children's friends have been non-members."

Still, it seems clear that the friends of the children generally have had an important positive influence on them, and 95 percent of the parents said they approved of their children's friends most of the time.

Among the 5 percent who registered a negative vote was a mother who told us in an interview, "Our children played with the most active families in our ward, but we found sometimes their influence was against observance of Church standards (for example, observing the Sabbath, no R-rated movies, no dating until sixteen). This resulted in a situation where we seemed to be the only family pushing for the observance of Church counsel."

One couple reported: "We had a lot of trouble with one daughter because of the friends she had. They had different values, and she was always in some sort of difficulty with them. As we talked about it, we decided to intervene more directly and encouraged her to have parties in our home to which she invited other girls. She sort of discovered that it was fun to have other friends—friends who reinforced family values rather than presenting her with conflicts."

When we asked parents whether children generally brought their friends home or instead went to their friends' homes, 34 percent answered "mostly in our home," 57 percent found the time divided about equally between friends' homes and their own home. Only 8 percent indicated that their children spent most of their time in the homes of their friends. A Utah mother of nine explained a family policy of discouraging the children from spending "a lot of time with friends outside of the family–there is an absolute prohibition on sleep-overs." This mother also noted that "our younger children possibly play more elsewhere than the older ones did because they don't have as many brothers and sisters at home." A Utah couple with six living children observed that the children mostly brought their friends home, except for one boy who "loves to be everywhere. Everyone is his family." One mother of six reflected, during an interview, mixed feelings about having her home as the neighborhood hand-out: "I was usually glad that our children's friends wanted to come to our home. It was fun to have lots of kids in the house—parties, music, talking. But I have to admit that sometimes I would wish that just some of the time they would go to somebody else's house besides ours. I would have liked to see some of the other mothers prepare the food or snacks and then clean up after everyone had gone home."

DATES

We did not ask specific questions about the children's dating patterns and partners; but, as we expected, a number of parents mentioned them. If they mentioned dating ages, it was usually to stress their insistence that the children wait until age sixteen to begin dating. Twenty-three percent of the parents identified peer influence and attractive influences outside the home as the factors that made it hardest to raise teenagers.

One Utah couple expressed real ambiguity about their youngest daughter's insistence on dating only Latinos. An elder sister had already undergone a divorce, and they were concerned about potential instability in another marriage. "We are trying to handle this situation with love, support, and non judgmental attitudes," they wrote. "They have all been fine young men, and we've included them in our family activities; but by so doing, we are in fact okaying the relationships. This a conflict for us." A California couple with three children was dismayed when their only daughter insisted on going steady through most of her high-school years against their wishes. They tried to handle the situation with "patience and love" rather than direct confrontation.

A Wyoming couple with seven children recalls "dating controversies" as a major form of adversity, which they tried to handle with "love and concern." An Idaho couple, also with seven children, considered a long-term relationship of one daughter's a major difficulty in their life. "They were going steady in high school and wanted to marry. We didn't want them to," they wrote. The parents' way of dealing with the situation was "patience and talking with the boy". "He spent so much time with her he felt like our son." The problem was resolved as the two teenagers "became very bored with each other and broke up, and our daughter went to college."

One couple felt that a beneficial rule for their teenagers had been that they could not own a motorized vehicle until after they left home. Although the children with licenses had generous access to the family car, this rule meant that parents continued to exercise a good deal of supervision over their whereabouts. Another couple held out firmly against the local popularity of dirt-bikes and motorcycles for the same reason. Other parents had driving-related rules: No driving until after driver's education; no driving for sons until they became Eagle Scouts; no driving if the grades slipped below a certain level; no driving without permission. Family members who drove had to help transport others. One couple wrote: "We found it was a great help in the family when the older children learned to drive. Then they could take the young ones to school, Church functions, seminary, ball games, and so on."

SIBLING INFLUENCE

We did not ask parents to compare the influence of friends with the influence of brothers and sisters, but we suspect that siblings would rate much higher than friends. Eighty-eight percent of the couples responded that their elder children were "very important" in training the younger children. Another 11 percent felt that they were "somewhat" important. Not a single couple checked "not at all important." One father, who had been raised in a family of twelve children, recalled that his own father had often said, "Mother and I reared the first six and then *they* reared the last six." He and his wife felt that their own children had followed much the same pattern.

This is how parents rated the influence of the elder children:

1. Being an example	97%
2. Attending functions when younger ones are participating	92%
3. Encouraging younger ones to study or work hard	80%
4. Helping with school work	75%
5. Writing letters of encouragement	57%
6. Helping prepare talks	40%
7. Playing with them and being a friend	40%

Comments on the "other" line included "sharing books they've enjoyed," "including young ones in many of their activities," "encouragement in Scouting, physical fitness, grooming, and manners," "teaching them dancing, piano, and songs," "passing their jobs from one to another and expecting them to do as well," "training them in sports," "helping them see the importance of the family and doing well," "playing together a lot, particularly in areas where the parents don't share the same interests," "playing ball with them," "being interested in each other's welfare," "being a good friend," and "participating in family activities even after they are married."

Many parents commented in one place or another that they consistently counted on the older children to tend the younger ones in their absence.

Several parents added comments about the influence of their children on each other. One mother remarked, "I don't know how we would have reared the younger children in the family without the great example of our eldest child. She had such a sweet, loving disposition and was always so helpful that all of the other children loved her and wanted to be like her. She made it easy for us to keep all the rest on the right path." A California mother of four observed that one of the most effective forms of discipline in their family was "pressure from other siblings to do what was right."

An Idaho couple with seven children discovered that the nature of discipline in their family had changed as the children grew older because the three older children actually did a great deal of parenting for the younger four. With a touch of humor, the mother wrote: "I asked our three older children how many rules we have and they said, 'Oh, lots! When we were little, anyway. Now there don't seem to be any for the younger four brothers and sisters.'"

When she asked the younger ones how many rules they had, they also answered, "Oh, lots." Then, she asked them to name some. They answered, "Oh, I guess 'to obey' is the only one."

"The older children feel that their father and I have really become less strict through the years—perhaps with some foundation in fact; although, if we did, it was unintentional. The younger children have the older children and their friends for examples as well as us. Many times as parents we've found ourselves taking sides with a younger child who has violated a rule; but when three or four siblings pounce on them for correction, the parents don't also need to pounce."

A Utah father of five closely spaced children recalled, "We soon discovered that we relied heavily on our eldest, a boy, to set the example and be responsible for the others. Like many other parents, we saw (too late to change much) that what we expected was a quantum leap more demanding than what we expected from the youngest. But the elder ones did look after the younger ones. They always went to the others' ball games or programs. They set the pattern for Church attendance, good grades, mission preparation, and general [obedience]."

Another father wrote, "I will always be grateful for the great example our eldest daughter set for the rest of the children. She had such a great spirit—never complained, pouted, or rebelled. We could count on her to get behind the things we were trying to accomplish. She worked hard in school, got good grades, and had a sensitive feeling for spiritual things. All of this rubbed off on the younger ones."

Only two couples indicated that older children could sometimes be negative examples. "In our family the older ones are so involved in themselves they don't always have time for anyone outside themselves," wrote one mother. A Texas couple with five children wrote, "Our older children were not always a good example, so the younger ones know what they should *not* do." One girl remarked, "I learned from the tough experiences my older brother had with our parents. He would get into trouble with the folks and I would learn what not to do."

HEROES

We asked about family heroes in an effort to determine whether parents deliberately selected people worthy of emulation and held them up as models for their children. In retrospect, we wished that we had specifically asked about "heroes and heroines," since almost no one identified women as role models. Our phrasing may have influenced parents to think only of men in their answers.

Also, by asking the parents, we excluded many individual models. It is possible that a whole different set of names would have emerged if we had asked the children to identify their own heroes. In fact, a few questionnaires specified "no family heroes" but listed people who were heroes for certain individuals or groups in the family. For instance, in one California family with four children, the twenty-one-year-old son had President Ronald Reagan as a hero, the twenty-two-year-old daughter had Marie Osmond, and the husband had Bob Hope.

The results are interesting. Forty-nine percent either said they had no family heroes or qualified the question is some way. For example, one Idaho couple wrote "There are many people we admire but no heroes." Another Idaho couple observed, "We respect our Church leaders, especially our bishop, but we don't have heroes." One couple identified the television program *M*A*S*H* as providing a family hero but did not specify which characters on the show they particularly enjoyed. A Montana couple with eight children identified as their family heroes "those who are righteously successful," while a Salt Lake City couple with five children said their family heroes were "strong, active, loving, friendly men in our ward."

When we analyzed who the listed heroes were—either as first or second choices—we got these results:

President Spencer W. Kimball	51%
Church leaders (as a group)	46%
Relatives	44%
Parents	42%
Sports figures	24%
Political leaders	18%
Jesus Christ	8%
Movie stars	8%

We found it interesting that family members are mentioned as heroes less often than President Kimball but more often than LDS athletes like Johnny Miller, Steve Young, and Danny Ainge.

One couple, who identified some ancestors as family heroes, explained: "We have had some fine grandparents who are really special to us. They were among the early converts to the Church, and they did a lot for our family in setting a good example. Their lives were not easy. Some of their little children were buried along the way West. They built a new home in a new area without assistance from anyone but the Lord. We don't need any hero from out in the world somewhere. We have great heroes in our own family."

In a family of four, the mother consulted the children on the question of heroes. "Our daughter said, 'Hannah Dustin'! She is an ancestor who was captured by Indians, scalped a great number of them, and helped others captured with her to escape. We visited her monument one year on vacation when our daughter was about eleven. Her brother, who was six at the time of this vacation, also mentioned Hannah. Other heroes are Spencer W. Kimball and John W. Hess, another ancestor."

A Montana couple with seven children wrote: "Husband likes LeGrand Richards. We all agree on Jesus Christ, Nephi, Joseph Smith, Moroni, President Kimball, and John Glenn. I'm sorry it's such a sarcastic world. It's hard to find someone contemporary to emulate." A Utah family for whom culture was important listed "great artists, authors, and musicians" among their heroes. An Idaho family with seven children observed, "We all follow BYU sports, but the children look up to their grandparents more than anyone we know. They were strong, exceptional people. Even the older married children talk of them and their ideals." A Utah couple wrote, "Jesus Christ is always mentioned as our model, yet to call him a hero is somewhat sacrilegious!" A Utah family with seven children listed Walt Disney, Nephi, and "pilots."

Another family had a long list: "Jesus Christ, President Kimball, a German soccer player, Kane in the TV series *Kung Fu*, Patriarch Copeland, the family in the *Little House on the Prairie*, Danny White, and Merlin Olsen."

Effective families do not exist in a vacuum. But they do seem to pay a great deal of attention to the values held by those who associate with their children. They also train their older children carefully. The payoff is that these older children almost always perpetuate the parents' values in dealing with the younger children so that the family can have a strong internal culture, a clear sense of "this is how we do things in our family." Friends have a generally positive influence on the children, probably because the children unconsciously, and for the most part, select friends with similar values, and partly because the family culture also affects these friends. The fact that almost 85 percent of family heroes are either other family members, Church authorities, or other Church members only reinforces the already strong pattern of family values.

CHAPTER ELEVEN

CHANGING YOUR FAMILY

Many Latter-day Saints who read this book might ask, "How can we become a more effective family?" You may have preschoolers and elementary school-age children; perhaps new babies are still coming. Or perhaps your children are teenagers or adults living at home. Regardless of your children's ages, parenting presents a variety of challenges. There is no particular age or stage when parenting is automatically easier. We asked the parents in our survey the four following questions:

1. At what age have you found your children the easiest to rear?
2. Why do you think that is?
3. At what age have you found your children the most difficult to rear?
4. Why do you think that is?

Sixteen percent of the parents responded that they had found all times equally easy, and 2 percent said they had never found an easy time. The remainder of respondent's answers made a pattern illustrated in the table below:

Age	Easiest to Rear	Hardest to Rear
0-5	26%	8%
6-12	37%	5%

13-15	9%	41%
16-18	3%	32%
19-21	3%	4%
over 21	2%	1%

It will surprise no one that 73 percent of the families identified the teen years as the hardest, although an interesting discovery was that the earlier teen years seem to involve more difficulties than the later teens. Even so, 12 percent of the parents found the teenage years the easiest of any stage.

When we asked the parents to give reasons for their answers, the pattern, again not surprisingly, revolved around authority and individualism, showing that Mormon families are not much different from American families in general. Twenty-six percent of the parents said that preschoolers were easiest to rear with 37 percent opting for the six-to-twelve age group. Of these parents, 40 percent cited, as the reason these ages were easier, the willingness of their children to accept guidance. Twenty-two percent gave as a reason that it was easier to talk things over with a younger child, who was more likely to accept the parent's reasoning. Fifty-nine percent of parents who said the teenage years were the hardest cited the child's increasing need for autonomy as the reason for the conflict. Twenty-three percent cited peer influence and outside activities as the reason these years were so difficult.

Many parents added comments on the questionnaire or during interviews about why they responded as they did. A Provo couple with eight children, ages seven to twenty-three, said that "all ages" were easy to rear because of their particular family structure: "The wife worked most with the children when they were younger, and the husband when they were older." They had two sons, a daughter, another son, and then four daughters, and they had checked that while both parents were equally responsible for teaching, helping, and disciplining the children between the ages of six and twelve, that the husband took over decisions about the duties and behavior of the boys after age six, while the wife continued to make most of the decisions about the duties and behavior of the girls.

A mother whose two children were born a year apart, when her husband's four children from his first marriage were between twelve and nineteen, acknowledged that, "Nothing but love and patience can build trust and unity in a step-parent situation. I find children absolutely fascinating and fun at each stage of development." The Idaho parents of ten children ranging in age from twelve to twenty-nine corroborated, "Every age has its special problems and its very special joys. Each child had a difficult period or so, but on the whole, we have thoroughly enjoyed every age of every child."

An Idaho mother of six children, ages sixteen to thirty-four, wrote, "Every year I wished that time would stand still. Raising children was such a wonderful joy and challenge. If I had to choose, I'd say the early teens were the hardest. The children had to become adults, and parents had to make the transition from rule givers to friends. It's a time for learning for all of us."

A Salt Lake City couple with three sons and three daughters, all of them married except for one daughter who was just completing a mission, observed, "There's no easy time. It's always a challenge." She added, "We enjoyed all ages. It's just that each age has different difficulties."

One couple from Idaho with two daughters and two sons between ages twenty-two and twenty-nine, all married, had very precise memories about hard and easy ages. "Six was easiest," they recalled, "because the world was more frightening to them and they were more willing to listen and seek parental help. Fifteen was hardest because of their wanting to be independent and because of peer pressure."

Some parents see the preschool years as easiest. The California parents of three living children wrote that the first year of life was easiest: "They were cuddly, cute, and cooperative."

Another mother, who also found the preschool years easiest, wrote: "In many respects, there was more work to be done when all of the children were little and we had two or three in diapers at the same time. But every day there was a quiet time when all of the children were in bed—bathed and looking so clean and sweetly asleep. We always knew pretty much where they were; and while there were quarrels and tiffs, we usually could settle things.

"Now that most of the children are teenagers, it's a different world. They want to be gone all the time, and we have to keep insisting that they tell us where they are going and when they will be back. They want to go places, do things, and wear things we don't feel too good about, but they say, 'Everyone else does it. Why can't we?'

"We know they get hurt or upset, but it isn't easy anymore to talk with them about their problems. When they were little, they brought every little problem or concern to us, but that has really changed. Dad and I often feel like strangers on the outside wanting to help but not knowing how to get in.

"We recall how we used to say we would be so thankful

when we got all the kids out of diapers, into school, and had some time to ourselves. But now I can see that those early years were really less complicated and worrisome than things are now."

Several couples like the ages from babyhood to two because they are less trouble than the other ages, but that seemed to be largely a matter of spacing. For example, one Provo couple with three children born in three years and a fourth four years later recalls those first three years as the most difficult "because we were most restricted. The father had less time because of being in school. We had less money. We got less sleep. The children demanded constant attention, and we had less freedom."

A Utah couple with nine children, ages eight to twenty-seven, likes ages six to twelve because these children "can care for themselves but they're still teachable and there isn't as much peer pressure. After fourteen, they found their children "testing rules, striving for independence, subject to peer pressure, and involved in proving themselves to their peers and to themselves." A Utah couple with fourteen children, ages seven to thirty, also consider the years between six and twelve easy. "They are beyond usual childhood diseases, and they haven't yet thought of dating, driving cars, and so on." A Provo couple with seven living children, ages twelve to twenty-nine, exuberantly wrote as the easiest age: "Six to twelve and twenty-plus! No diapers and no teenagers!"

One Utah father with five sons, ages twenty-two to thirty with two married, observed: "The golden years in our family were the teenage period. Our fourth child was born when the first was turning five, and our fifth arrived three years later. My recollection of those early years is one of lots of work, sick kids, and heavy physical demands. For about five of those years, I was a bishop or had heavy church responsibilities, and my wife had a great deal of work and responsibility.

"However, when the boys were all teenagers, they could either drive or go with someone besides the parents. Everything seemed to happen at our house—parties, song practices, play rehearsals, and student body election committee meetings. Loud music was always competing with somebody on the guitar or piano. The food bill was astronomical. We spent all of our time going to ballgames, plays, and programs. I loved it.

"And there were never any real problems with our children. There were the usual romances and breakups, lost elections and football games, a constant hassle about neglected chores; but we did a lot of things together—skiing, fishing, golfing, ballgames, and great family trips and vacations. We liked being together, and the talk was always rich and stimulating. Underneath it all was the knowledge that in just a few years our boys would all be on missions. We savored the crowded years that were passing so rapidly. At least in my mind, these years were the easiest."

CONDITIONS NECESSARY FOR CHANGE

Even if change is desirable, is it possible? One Montana couple had each been raised in inactive homes and did not become active themselves until the first four of their seven children were already in their teens. They saw the absence of Church influence in those early years as crucial. One son had run away several times. A second preferred non-Mormon friends. One son had served a mission and married in the temple, but his brother and the two daughters had not. The contrast with the younger children, they felt, was marked. Do the experiences in this family prove that change is impossible if a family wants to alter an original direction? Not necessarily. A great deal of research has been done on how and why people change. Two conditions seem to be absolutely essential for change to occur, as is explained in the following paragraphs.

People change only when *they feel a strong need to change*. Research has looked at religious conversion, management training, Weight-Watchers, and Alcoholics Anonymous and has reached this conclusion. Unless people "sign up" feeling powerfully, even desperately, that they need to change, just sitting through the program and going through the motions won't affect a change. Before a family can change, at least one person in that family has to say, "We cannot let our family continue to go on as it has. Things aren't right. I'm going to do absolutely everything in my power to help make things better."

People change when someone they respect agrees with them and supports the change. Alcoholics Anonymous assigns each person a "buddy" who has overcome the same problem and who will be on call for as long as the person needs help. If the wife is the one who feels that something has to change, the husband, too, needs to support the change. Then if the couple has a friend, parent, bishop, or home teachers who can give support, encouragement, or suggestions, the chances for success increase further.

Newly converted parents often pray for the first time

with a missionary who gives a model for prayer and also serves as an authority figure in asking for the prayer to be said. Both parents and children accept family prayer because they accept the new teaching situation. In other words, this family has both social support and a person to initiate the change–learning to pray. In a family setting, the parents must usually initiate any change; but usually they can do this simply by announcing they are going to change something, or better still, holding a family discussion about what needs to change and how.

"How" is important. It is not enough for a couple to say, "We need to start talking together more." A more effective plan would be for parents to decide: "We are going to do three things: (1) Every night before the children go to bed, we will all meet in our bedroom, talk about the day's events or things coming up, or share some memories of times past, and then have family prayer together. (2) We parents will make a list of gospel topics and questions. During Sunday dinner, you children can choose one of these topics for discussion, or you may take a turn telling the rest of us what you learned in church that day. We'll tell what we learned, too. (3) On Fast Sunday (or another specified time during the month), father will have a personal interview with each child. During the interview they will talk about any concerns the child has, any issues the parents want to raise, and goals that the child wants to set."

If the program is this clear, if everyone in the family agrees on it, and if the parents are willing to put the energy into seeing that it actually happens every day, every week, every month, then change will come.

A real roadblock to change is the amount of effort it takes. People simply get tired of putting all the necessary effort into a project long enough for the new pattern to feel comfortable. Also, most people are afraid of failing or looking inept when they try something new. One father ruefully reported what happened when he tried making a change: "I was not satisfied with the degree of closeness we had in our family. We didn't talk together or do much together. We all seemed to be going in different directions. I was determined to bring the family closer and had an image of our family enjoying lively discussions together. So I told my wife and our three children (ages nine, twelve, and fourteen) that I wanted everyone to be at dinner promptly that evening. We were all going to sit around and have a good time talking. When they weren't at the table on time, I yelled at everyone and finally got them seated. Then I asked my son,

'What did you do today at school?'

'Nothing.'

'Anything interesting happen?'

'Nope.'

I got the same non-response from the rest of the kids. The phone rang and they all jumped up to get it, and I decided to forget the whole thing."

Similarly, if a family has never held a family home evening before, the parents may feel very anxious about trying this new activity. Because the children will be resisting change for exactly the same reason, the anxiety has some justification. One father in an active family that conscientiously tried to have a regular family home evening revealed some of the problems: "There's an old saying in the Church that family home evening is the only fight that is opened and closed with prayer. That isn't exactly how our family night sessions are, but they aren't as effective as my wife and I would like. First, one or more of the kids is often busy and either doesn't want to have family night or wants to cut it short. Then the age differences among the children sometimes make it difficult to get everyone interested in a topic. I think our best lessons have been those where the children give the lesson to the rest of the family."

The next problem is how to get the children behind the change, not just putting up with it to accommodate mom and dad. In addition to just plain sticking with it until dinner-table conversation becomes a habit, how can you encourage children to invest in the activity and see that they too are benefiting from it?

One way is to keep the goal clear. Say, "I really enjoy dinnertime now. I enjoy learning what you kids thought about Brother Miller's talk. I feel that we're learning to communicate better as a family." Or make the topic of conversation clear enough that the "rules" for participation are clear: "Jane told me something very interesting about alternative energy forms that they discussed in school today. Why don't you tell them about it, Jane? Do you have any ideas, Stan, on which forms might be most practical in this area?"

Another suggestion is to reward people for their participation: "I really appreciate Bart's suggestion that we broaden the topics to include current events. I thought at first that we needed to concentrate on gospel topics; but they have a way of creeping into everything anyway."

Deal with resistance and negative behavior in terms of the goal, not the person: "Rob, we've all decided that we want to improve how our family communicates. When you call Susan "a nerd" because she likes the president, does that help our family or hurt it? What will you do to help?"

Let the children articulate their feelings about what's happening as they work toward the goal: "Susan, you and Rob had quite a debate about the president tonight, and in the past, that's been quite a sore point between you sometimes. How did you feel about tonight's discussion?"

CASE STUDIES

In light of these suggestions, let us share with you two case studies of Latter-day Saint families that made a decided change. We've altered the names and certain other information to safeguard their privacy.

Jack grew up in a community just outside of Salt Lake City in a solid working-class family known as good Latter-day Saints, even though the father worked most Sundays and attended church irregularly. Jack was active while he was growing up, but when he enlisted in the navy at seventeen for World War II, he was never stationed near a branch. Naturally, he could not attend church. None of his new companions were Latter-day Saints, and he went along with them, drinking coffee and occasionally drinking liquor with them on shore leave.

Discharged at age twenty, Jack went back home and found that most of his high school friends were also inactive. He didn't go back to church. After several months, he met Betty, and they began dating seriously. She was an active Church member from an active family, but she fell in love. To her parents' disappointment, she married Jack outside the temple.

Jack and Betty moved to another community in the Salt Lake City area. Jack was ambitious and hard working. He took a weekend job and also started to build their house on weekends. For more than eight years, Betty went to meetings periodically, but Jack was a virtual stranger in the ward.

They had four sons; and as the boys got old enough to attend Primary and Sunday School, Jack and Betty began to have a series of talks together about their future as a family. These talks were largely initiated by Betty. They discussed at length what they wanted for their sons. For both, it included active Church membership.

During their entire marriage, Jack and Betty knew that Jack's mother and Betty's parents hoped they would return to activity in the Church. They never criticized or pressured Jack and Betty, but Jack always knew that they would be deeply pleased if he became active again. And he knew it was mostly up to him, because Betty was already quite committed to activity.

While Jack and Betty were having these discussions, the elders quorum president in their ward began to visit them, encouraging Jack to attend priesthood meetings with him. Betty and Jack both respected him and considered him a friend, so Jack somewhat reluctantly accepted the invitation and began to attend more regularly. As his confidence grew, he was asked to teach a Sunday School class, and he accepted.

Then Jack was offered an attractive job in another part of the state, and the family moved to a new location. They might have drifted back into inactivity, but their new bishop noticed that they had two boys who were of Cub Scout age and called Betty to be a den mother and Jack a cubmaster.

Soon they were thoroughly involved in the ward. They agreed to attend a Project Temple series, again at the bishop's invitation, and were sealed in the temple. Other ward positions came for both of them. Jack was called as a counselor in the bishopric, then as bishop. After a long time in this key position, he was made a member of the stake high council. Betty served in several auxiliary positions and then in the stake Relief Society presidency. Three of their four boys filled missions, and all married in the temple.

Jack and Betty had turned their lives around and made a permanent difference in the lives of their children. All of the elements were present to encourage and support change. Jack and Betty felt a deep need to make a change. The elders quorum president gave a Jack a specific invitation to attend meetings in his company and with his approval. This man was present to ease the shock of returning to activity, and he supported Jack emotionally. Jack's mother and Betty's parents were openly delighted and very supportive.

The children had been attending Primary and Sunday School, so the change was not drastic for them. And, because they were young, they were very willing to go along with the decision of their parents.

As Jack and Betty became more active, they were rewarded by feeling more integrated into the ward, they developed a wider circle of friends, and they accepted positions that gave them more support, more status, and more positive reinforcement. At some point, they were fully active, not for the sake of their sons, but because they themselves were benefiting from their activity in the Church and fully believed in what they were doing. Going to the temple not only rewarded them with the knowledge that their family was now sealed forever, if they would continue worthy, but also articulated new covenants of devotion to the gospel.

The youthful ages of Jack and Betty's sons were certainly an advantage for them in making the change, but in the second case study, Scott and Paula needed to make the change operate effectively for their *teenage* children as well as themselves. Scott came from a very strong Latter-day Saint family and was a returned missionary. Paula's family was inactive. She attended Brigham Young University because it was convenient, and there the two met, fell in love, and married. They then they moved to California, and had four sons.

Scott attended church fairly regularly and held a few positions, while Paula was almost completely inactive. She smoked, drank coffee, and had an occasional cocktail. Despite her inactivity, their boys were baptized at eight and attended church with Scott.

Then one Sunday when their oldest boy was about sixteen and the youngest was nine, the stake president phoned asked Scott to come to his office and bring Paula. With some foreboding, Scott agreed. The stake president told them that their ward was being divided, and the new bishop wanted Scott to be one of his counselors. Would Scott accept the call and would Paula support him? Scott answered, "President, I am honored to receive this call, but my wife and I are not worthy." The stake president looked at both of them and asked, "You can get worthy, can't you?" Scott and Paula looked at each other and, with the ability married couples gain through the years, communicated with each other and agreed. Scott replied, "Yes, President, we can and will get worthy, and we accept the call."

In a daze they went home, called their sons around them, and told them of the new call. The boys were delighted and enthusiastic. They talked for some time about the changes all of them would have to make to be worthy of this new calling. Paula pledged never to use coffee, tea, alcohol, or tobacco again. They all agreed to start having prayer, going to church together, paying a full tithe, and having family home evening.

Making the decision was the easy part. Scott, the most religiously trained partner in the marriage, was gone a great deal with his new calling, leaving Paula, who was less experienced, to carry out many of the decisions. Sometimes they forgot. Sometimes they weren't prepared. Both Scott and Paula were determined to make the changes, however, and after several weeks the new activities became routine and began to feel "normal." Within a year Paula was called to serve in the ward Primary presidency. Their eldest son turned mission age and accepted a mission call. His three brothers followed in his footsteps. The family became one of the stake stalwarts. Paula found she enjoyed the temple and attended frequently. Later she became stake Relief Society president, and Scott served on the high council.

This family was truly transformed. For Scott and Paula, the need to change was stimulated by an important new Church calling. Both the bishop and the stake president were important people giving support and encouragement. All of the boys rallied around the decision and provided the needed family social support. All these things made the change happen.

These two case studies happen to be success stories. There is no guaranteeing older children will support a change, even when the parents are totally behind it; but it is certain that weak commitment and uncertainty on the part of the parents will doom change before it begins.

One father talked about his reluctance to start a needed change. He said, "We have never had family prayer in our home. I feel it would be a great strength to all of us if we started this practice. But I don't know how to begin. I'm afraid that if I try it, my kids will all snicker and make fun of the whole idea. After all, they have never even heard me pray aloud, and I don't know how anyone would react." His fears are not unrealistic, but it is doubtful he will be able to get anything started, if he continues to feel the way he does.

A possible approach might be: "Children, when I grew up we used to have family prayer in our home every morning and evening. The same thing happened in your mother's home. For some reason we just didn't get prayer started in our home. Mother and I have talked about it, and we want to begin to have family prayers together in our home. We would like to do this just before we eat breakfast and before dinner at night. We hope that all of you will come and kneel with us so we can have prayer together. This will help us as a family. We love each of you and want to do what is right."

If nothing else, the record of the highly effective families in this study should encourage parents about the possibility of changing. Parents of nine children, ranging in age from thirteen to twenty-nine, wrote: "We are trying with all our hearts to be an eternal family, and we do this unitedly. Even though we do not succeed always, we are trying. Inch by inch, day by day, line upon line, we shall continue to strive for that greatest of all goals—being an eternal family and having exaltation." The keys identified in this study appear to be moving them in the direction they desire to go.

CHAPTER TWELVE

FACING THE FUTURE

Since doing this research, we've talked with many young Mormon couples who are engaged, newly married, or first-time parents. They ask us if our research applies to them. The world they face seems very different from that of our two hundred families, whose children are either launched on their own or are within a few years of leaving.

We think our research *does* apply to these young couples; but they must consider that they are different from our survey families in many ways. What are some of these differences?

The percentage of converts in the Church is steadily growing larger. Will these numbers tip the Mormon tradition toward more "worldly" values when it comes to raising strong, Church-centered families? In our opinion, this should not be a major challenge. Mormons did not invent strong families. Almost every religious tradition enhances and encourages family life. And despite the bad press on families, the institution of the family is still—and probably always will be—a prime American value as well.

The Church doesn't have all the good families. Alarm about the "disappearing" American family, or about the family slipping into a slough of greedy materialism, seems decidedly misplaced. Furthermore, building better families will probably get more national emphasis in the years ahead. Converts who come from strong families will find in the Church only support for values they already espouse.

"Strong" does not necessarily mean "traditional." Currently, fewer than 25 percent of American families fit into the pattern of a full-time homemaker/mother and full-time wage-earning father. In younger families especially, both couples are likely to be employed and also share child-care and homemaking responsibilities; this division of labor is far from equally shared in most cases, and the woman is usually most heavily burdened. In such cases, couples must usually make a decision to have fewer children or to have at least one parent at a time limit his or her career to spend more time with the children. Although research is far from final on dual-career couples, parents who have the energy, resources, and commitment *are* able to provide high-quality parenting and simultaneously maintain satisfying careers. Probably more and more young couples will move into this pattern, although some who are not suited for it by personality will be forced into it by economic necessity.

By far the greatest increase, however, has been single-parent families. Approximately eleven million American children—20 percent of the nation's youngsters—are currently being raised by their mother alone. Another 1 million are being raised by their father alone. Sixty percent of black children and 33 percent of white children have divorced parents.

Latter-day Saints who marry in the temple have a divorce rate of 6 percent, while 30 percent of Mormons married out of the temple have been divorced. Nationally, 23 percent of "ever married" people have been divorced.

About 65 percent of all Latter-day Saint households have a married couple in them, while about 35 percent are single adult households without children. About 4 percent of Latter-day Saint households consist of children and a single parent.

All of this means a shift in the traditional pattern of the family. Parents will be under much greater pressure to plan for the time they have available for their children, particularly if they are parenting without partners. As this study shows, mothers have spent more time with the children than the fathers have—talking with them, checking on direction and problems, monitoring situations, and acting as an early warning system to bring the father's attention to bear on problems that the mother spots. In the future, both parents, not just the mother, will need to spend quality time with the children and make family activities their highest priority. Even though work may still take the largest portion of time, the most creative and energetic thought should be spent on family life.

If two working parents (or a single parent) come home, exhausted, to children who have been doing nothing but watching television since after school ,and then sink down in front of their own favorite programs, the patterns that build effective families could be in jeopardy. Parents who are too tired to attend church, or too pinched financially to pay tithing, or too busy to have family prayer will not be able to teach these values to their children.

Our data show that most LDS parents exercise some control over their children's television habits, either directly or by teaching them what constitutes appropriate viewing, and make schoolwork a high priority. Will busy parents allow children to watch more television as a way of freeing up time for themselves? If so, consider the results if "media values" become the most dominant in the home.

Another real problem is complacency. Bill is president of a Brigham Young University stake. Over the past five years, attendance at sacrament meeting has remained constant; but attendance at priesthood meeting, Sunday School, and Relief Society has declined steadily, along with home teaching and visiting teaching. When we talk to students about these trends, some frankly describe lessons from Church manuals as boring, and some Church programs as irrelevant; but far more serious and more frequent is the "it doesn't matter" feeling. "There's no real reason for me to feel that being active is essential," observed one. "The Church is so strong here that what I do or don't do doesn't make a difference to it." Others added, "Besides, everyone misses some meetings or goes to an R-rated movie. It's no big deal."

While we might agree about the quality of certain lessons or the lack of earthshaking consequences for going to an occasional R-rated movie, what we do see very clearly is that relativity is a slippery slide. Young people who don't have clear boundaries on their behavior, who keep waffling about what is or isn't important, can be backed over the edge into serious transgression in a remarkably short period of time. Furthermore, will these people who face no immediate dire consequences, have firm convictions as parents about what is right and wrong? Will they have the will to pass these values on to their children?

Another difference for the future is family size. The couples in our study averaged six children apiece. The average number of children born to Latter-day Saint families is now 3.3 compared to just over 2 for the average American family. There seems to be some evidence that

Latter-day Saint families are following the national trend downward. What differences might this trend make?

We can make some guesses. Parents with six children obviously cannot do all the work themselves. No matter how hard it is to get children to do chores, the children have to help. Also, with six children to provide for, the family income is stretched thin. For extra money, children must take jobs outside the family or work for what they get within it. If parents have smaller families, will they still have the same motivation and need to teach their children the work ethic?

According to our data, Mormon families are already concerned about keeping a nice home, going on vacations, and doing things together. Right now, these factors reflect the parents' emphasis on achieving greater family unity. It is possible, however, that they could be seen as ends in themselves rather than as means to an end. If so, family unity may be one of the casualties of a more materialistic life-style.

Does this mean that we, as sociologists, advise young couples to plan a traditional marriage? Not necessarily. Certainly, we feel that the traditional model is an option that young couples should have available if they wish to make that choice and can sustain its demands. Certainly, there is nothing "easy" about a traditional marriage, any more than there is about a nontraditional marriage. However, we are not advising young people to choose that model without looking at it carefully, weighing its pros and cons, and considering other options as well.

We see no virtue in poverty for its own sake. We've seen too often how financial tensions can absorb nearly all the emotional energies of a couple until there is nothing left to enrich the relationship. Negative consequences are likely in a scenario where the husband is so concerned about providing for his family that he has neither time nor energy left over for parenting, and where the wife, who is having a baby every two years, is increasingly isolated in caring for the children largely by herself. It is usually the wife whose academic interests and training get put on hold, sometimes permanently, for the sake of the family. We see a great potential for happy family life in a pattern that allows—even insists—that both parents get to develop both their nurturing sides and their achieving sides simultaneously.

However, making this pattern work effectively will require a degree of intelligence, awareness, and flexible planning as the family moves from stage to stage, more so than in previous generations. The traditional pattern has worked and worked well largely because the assignment of tasks made it possible to keep the bases covered. If tasks and roles have to be renegotiated every three to six months because of inevitable shifts in the family situation or activities, families are looking at an enormous amount of work—too much to be worth it. Actually, acquiring communication skills, being aware of individual family members' needs, and choosing time after time to put family values and Church service first over other demands cannot help but have the same good results we see in highly effective traditional families. However, each family must decide what works best for them and their unique situation.

We have every reason to believe that families of the future might respond quite differently to a questionnaire such as ours that asks questions about activities, money, education, and chores. But we suspect that the answers about family strengths, family values, and feelings for each other would be just about the same. The task of building a strong family is one that has to be undertaken by each couple, no matter how successful or unsuccessful their own families were.

Our scenario for the future involves diversity. The principles of family building as emphasized by our Church leaders and described in Church magazines and lessons are still the same, but the actual forms into which these principles are translated are changing. We see not just one image of a successful family but many. We see a pattern of increasing pluralism, where the emphasis is not on roles but on skills—the same skills of communicating, teaching gospel principles, and developing competence at a variety of tasks that successful families in this study have discovered.

Despite the ugly side of our society—violence, moral transgression, and materialism—it supports some family values in a way that earlier American society did not. It stresses problem solving, not just problem enduring. It puts a high value on communication skills. It recognizes the real satisfactions of achievement. It emphasizes planning and taking charge of the future. These societal values can and will reinforce important gospel values for thoughtful, sensitive parents who are committed to each other and to their children.

We, the authors, we've completed most of our parenting, but we're cheering for our children as they, in turn, become parents. In some ways, we envy them. The future is going to be an exciting time to build strong families, and we wish them—and you—joy in the process.